Ready to Launch

How Prepared are they for the Real World?

———————————————

Dina Renee Weiss and Brett Pawelkiewicz

© 2016

Copyright ©2016 The Village LLC

All rights reserved. No part of this book may be reproduced, stored or introduced into a retrieval system, or transmitted in any form or by any means (electronic, mechanical, photocopying, recording or otherwise), without the prior written permission of the publisher of this book. The scanning, uploading, or distribution of this book via the Internet or via any other means without the permission of the publisher is illegal and punishable by law.

Ready to Launch
How Prepared are they for the Real World?
by Dina Renee Weiss and Brett Pawelkiewicz

Edited by Marti A. Lucia
Photos by Dina Renee Weiss
Design by The Village LLC

LIMIT OF LIABILITY/DISCLAIMER OF WARRANTY: WHILE THE PUBLISHER AND AUTHOR HAVE USED THEIR BEST EFFORTS IN PREPARING THIS BOOK, THEY MAKE NO REPRESENTATIONS OR WARRANTIES WITH RESPECT TO THE ACCURACY OR COMPLETENESS OF THE CONTENTS OF THIS BOOK AND SPECIFICALLY DISCLAIM ANY IMPLIED WARRANTIES OF MERCHANTABILITY OR FITNESS FOR A PARTICULAR PURPOSE. NO WARRANTY MAY BE CREATED OR EXTENDED BY SALES REPRESENTATIVES OR WRITTEN SALES MATERIALS. THE ADVICE AND STRATEGEIS CONTAINED HEREIN MAY NOT BE SUITABLE FOR YOUR SITUATION. YOU SHOULD CONSULT WITH A PROFESSIONAL WHERE APPROPRIATE. NEITHER THE PUBLISHER NOR AUTHOR SHALL BE LIABLE FOR ANY LOSS OF PROFIT OR ANY OTHER COMMERCIAL DAMAGES, INCLUDING BUT NOT LIMITED TO SPECIAL, INCIDENTAL, CONSEQUENTIAL OR OTHER DAMAGES.

International Standard Book Number: 978-0-692-78794-6

Printed in the United States of America

1 2 3 4 5 6 7 8 9 10

Dedication

To my kids, Cassidy and Jordan – may your launch lead to your greatest success in life, and still keep you within traveling distance…
– Dina Renee Weiss

To my siblings, Nick, Scott, Brad, Jordan, Megan, Jack and Lexi; my parents, Paul, Lisa and John; my grandparents, Ronald and Jean Pawelkiewicz and John and Karen Kamin; and to the memory of my great-grandparents, Ronald and Ruth Shafer
– Brett Pawelkiewicz

Ready to Launch

Table of Contents

Glossary of Terms 1

Preface 4

Introduction 5

Section 1 – Setting up the Household Corporation 7
    The Head Honcho
    The Pecking Order
    Vision Statement

Section 2 – The Job 26
    The Job Description
    Wages
    Resume, Please
    The Interview Process
    The Job Offer
    First Day on the Job: Orientation

Section 3 – Running the Corporation 80
    Reviews
    Correction and Discipline
    Tattletale Box
    Keeping Morale High
    Outside Business Activities
    Bonus Opportunities

Section 4 – Fiscal Responsibility – Earning, Spending and Saving......122
    Cash Flow, Budgeting and Goal-Setting

Table of Contents

Saving, Matching and Vesting

Investing

Credit

Section 5 – Preparing for a Household Corporation "Spin-Off" 161

If your kid is about ready to launch, you might want to read this section first!

Ready to Launch

Failure to Launch

Section 6 – Writing the Real Deal Resume 171

Appendix

Job Descriptions

Smith Household Kitchen Maintenance I

Smith Household Laundry Manager

Performance Review Worksheets

Director Evaluation Worksheet

Employee Evaluation Worksheet

Employee Self-Evaluation Worksheet

Priority Request Form

Savings Match and Vesting Worksheet

Special Thanks

Glossary of Terms

While most authors elect to bury their glossary of terms at the back of the book, we wanted to be sure that anyone reading this becomes quickly familiar with some of the terms we use, as well as our conversational and hopefully somewhat humorous tone. Incidentally, each of these terms is more accurately defined later in the book. ☺

Allowance. Money given regularly to a person for doing nothing in the hopes that they will stop asking for money.

Baseline duties. Stuff you just have to do for the benefit of being allowed to live at home. You do not deserve to get paid for these.

Cherry-Picking. Term used in both the farming as well as the investment industry, this is the practice of showing only your best stuff to a potential customer. By the way, it's illegal in the investment industry.

Corporate Spin-off. The official Launch of a seasoned wage earner.

Director. An Officer of the Household Corporation, the Director is at the top of the food chain and ultimately responsible for structuring and maintaining the flow of the things. The Director may also be known in certain circles as the Head Honcho, the Big Cheese, the Top Dog or simply Mom or Dad.

Dunce Phone. Also known as a flip-phone; the antiquated and decidedly uncool dunce phone harkens back to a time when cell phones were *not* smart and could only be used for phone calls and text messages and the only App that existed was *Snake*.

Financial Officer. Another Officer of the Household Corporation, the Financial Officer controls the money (all of the money…).

Free Lunch. Seriously, there is no such thing.

Hierarchy. We also refer to this as the Pecking Order and it represents who gets to tell who what to do.

Household Corporation. Less of a Family Business and more just the business of being a family.

Job Duties. These are the duties you get paid for.

Layaway. Very popular in the 1970s, well before the global credit crisis, this used to be the common sense way to buy something over time, without incurring any interest.

Match Forfeiture. What happens when the Laundry Manager loses one sock, or if you elect to pull matched money out of your savings too soon, you no longer get to keep it.

Matching Program. While this may sound like a way to coordinate an outfit, it is in fact what all the cool companies do; they offer you free money to go with the money you are saving for later.

Operations Manager. Yet another Officer of the Household Corporation, the Operations Manager picks up where the Director leaves off and essentially wears the back half of the horse costume.

Outside Business Activity. While not always done *outdoors*, an Outside Business Activity may be any job performed for a wage outside of the Household, like mowing lawns, running a lemonade stand or taking on a job at a fast food restaurant as a way to earn some extra scratch.

Proper Hygiene. What makes it proper is the adherence to strict standards like humming Happy Birthday in its entirety twice while brushing teeth or lathering, rinsing and repeating.

Qualifying Events. What makes you so special? Um, the fact that I'm 16 and can now drive...? A qualifying event is a milestone reached that grants the individual some special privilege or *qualifies* them for say, a job as Transportation Manager.

Glossary of Terms

The Real World. This does not refer to the reality show but is instead to the world outside of the home in which every parent lives and into which every wage earner will eventually launch.

Vesting. A schedule that has nothing to do with fashion, but instead determines when you have access to money saved outside the home, like in a bank, without having to give it up.

Vision Statement. A collectively-designed family goal that should be taped to the refrigerator and referred to any time someone thinks the rules do not apply to them.

Wage. What the Financial Officer offers to pay you.

Wage Earner. A collective of one to, well, more than one kid who are willing to accept a few bucks to do some meaningful work for the family.

Wage Premium. How much *more* the Financial Officer will pay you to do something seen as unpleasant for one reason or another.

> *"Building a strong foundation in the early years of a child's life will not only help him or her reach their full potential but will also result in better societies as a whole."*
> – Novak Djokovic, Professional Tennis Player

Preface

Educating kids on earning, saving, budgeting and spending money wisely is essential to their growth as individuals as well as to their success and financial stability in the future. Many parents and teachers do not possess the knowledge or ability to adequately teach young folks these skills, as they themselves may not know how to navigate these often complex and overwhelming topics. As such, the cycle continues and inasmuch as parents generally wish their kids could benefit from the lessons learned from their own mistakes, few are willing to admit to having made them, and many may not even recognize having done so.

This is not to say that parents and teachers are not financially savvy! It is only to provide a backdrop for this book, which is intended to bring guidelines, interest and even perhaps some fun to this type of education. It is our hope that in reading this book, parents, teachers and even those young folks we are ultimately seeking to help educate will learn valuable skills with respect to developing a strong work ethic, a commitment to self and success, and the basics and beyond surrounding personal financial planning and stability. And who knows, perhaps those parents and teachers may gain a tip or two along the way.

Introduction

We recently had the opportunity to speak to several eighth grade classes on saving and investing, and in doing so, posed the question, "who here gets an allowance?" In each class throughout the day, a percentage of the kids raised their hands, and that opened a discussion on earning, spending and saving money. A number of kids did receive an allowance, and interestingly enough, several kids across the course of day were even routinely employed (many of the kids work on family farms or have reliable babysitting jobs). As a follow-up, it was asked what those kids did with the money they earned, given that the impetus for our being brought in as guest lecturers was a three-month stock market project in which the kids participated. Only a very small number of kids (in fact, just two out of 200, or a paltry 1%) said they saved their money. One was saving for college, while the other was saving for designer fashion. Regardless of their priorities or specific financial goals for their money, there were only two savers, and both of them were employed rather than receiving an allowance. Interestingly enough, of those who *were* receiving an allowance, few could tell us what they had done to earn those dollars.

When turning to the great Merriam-Webster for a definition of the term allowance, the first "simple" definition listed is: "an amount of money that is given to someone regularly or for a specific purpose." The key word there is given. We feel that herein lies the problem. Over the years, and in the personal experience of at least one of the authors of this book, the practice of giving money to kids, rather than having them earn their financial reward, is common. The level and consistency of work and responsibility tied to those dollars, however, has proven random at best. As such, we are going to start by proposing a whole new way of looking at the dollars being given to our kids – one that might foster a sense of work ethic, commitment to the family and/or household, and if we are lucky, a keen understanding of how life will work once those kids grow beyond the lifestyle and responsibility of the home in which they are raised.

It is our hope that people from all walks of life, backgrounds and families will benefit from this book, and while we agreed it would be exhaustive to attempt to outline each possible household circumstance, we thought it might make sense to at least show two different types of households – so we are going to use the Smith Household and the Jones Household throughout the book.

Whether and how far you carry these ideas into the framework of your own household is entirely your prerogative. This book is not meant to teach you how to raise your kids or how to run a company, but rather to help your kids become financially savvy through learning the fundamental tenets of fiscal responsibility, the importance of a strong work ethic, the value in volunteering, and ultimately becoming a contributing member of society.

Let us introduce the concept of the Household Corporation…

Section 1

Setting up the Household Corporation

"Every successful individual knows that his or her achievement depends on a community of persons working together."

– Paul Ryan, 54th Speaker of the U.S. House of Representatives

Whether we realize it or not, households are essentially run as small businesses. Consider that all households have an operating budget, monthly and annual profits and losses, fixed and periodic expenses (often including capital expenditures, which may occur at random intervals), ongoing routine tasks that need completion, and a pecking order of responsibility and respect, to name a few. Some households are very simple and streamlined, with just one individual (i.e., yourself), one income, and a series of set expenses and responsibilities, while others prove to be much more complex, as in the case where there is more than one wage earner, one or more children, a larger number of daily household tasks, and a very busy schedule. Running any type of household is truly a big responsibility. Running the multi-person household often proves confusing or frustrating, with the significant probability of arguments or hurt feelings arising due to confusion or disagreements about who is in charge of what.

While it is not our intention to recreate a simplified MBA curriculum here, a small and succinct lesson in business administration and setting up the backbone for a successful corporation is. Spending a day on Wikipedia or perhaps even reading a book about the structure and organization of IBM might prove helpful; however, given that we would prefer you keep reading this particular book, we will go ahead and get started on what goes into structuring most operations.

The Head Honcho

Regardless of whether the officers of your Household Corporation will have actual titles, it is important for the corporate hierarchy that everyone know who is ultimately in charge. The officers serve in those roles. Every Household Corporation should, at a minimum, have a Director or CEO – for the purposes of this book, we are using the term Director to mean the top banana, the head honcho, or in some cases, Mom or Dad.

While not every Household Corporation will have enough people to staff each officer role individually, it is essential that the function of each role is understood in order to ensure that all those duties are being handled by someone, even if that someone is the same individual.

Duties that need to be covered and their assignment to the roles of each officer are reflected below:

DIRECTOR
- ✓ Determines what jobs need to be completed in the household
- ✓ Manages job postings
- ✓ Accepts resumes
- ✓ Interviews wage earners for potential job positions

- ✓ Sets the wage for each individual job, based upon budget and cash flow conversations with the financial officer
- ✓ Sets the protocol for handling unclaimed job postings
- ✓ Conducts performance reviews

FINANCIAL OFFICER
- ✓ Manages the finances and tracks profitability of the Household Corporation
- ✓ Tracks income and cash flow for the Household Corporation
- ✓ Sets the Household Corporation annual operating budget
- ✓ Sets wages for each individual job based on the Household Corporation's ability to make good on salaries earned on an ongoing basis
- ✓ Sets and manages the vesting schedule for savings and investment accounts
- ✓ Manages the savings and investments accounts for the wage earners
- ✓ Offers advice on savings programs based on individual goals as outlined with the Human Resources Manager
- ✓ Determines if there are surplus funds at year end for annual profit sharing contributions and bonus dollars, if applicable to your Household Corporation financial program
- ✓ Reviews with Director any proposed funding requests for various wage earner Outside Business Activities

OPERATIONS MANAGER

- ✓ Coordinates the schedules of all wage earners and sets the days on which various jobs need to be completed in order to maintain the harmonious flow of all household activities
- ✓ Coordinates the schedule of all extracurricular and social activities to allow time for various tasks and events (if a wage earner has an overbooked schedule and keeps letting their duties fall by the wayside, it is the job of the Operations Manager to determine whether a performance review is in order, even if it is not a scheduled one)
- ✓ Coordinates transportation
    - ✓ Determines which days transportation is available, and if, for instance, transportation to/from grocery store is only available on Saturday, this individual informs the Meal Planning Assistant they must have grocery list prepared for that trip
    - ✓ Arranges for everyone to get to their designated social, extracurricular, athletic, or even volunteer engagements

HUMAN RESOURCES MANAGER

- ✓ Develops team and wage earner benefits and opportunities centered on keeping morale high among all Household members
- ✓ Fields and responds to positive input as well as complaints from all Household members
- ✓ Structures, manages and dispenses all disciplinary measures
- ✓ Offers resources/training for optimal time management

- ✓ Provides assistance in determining an extracurricular "career" path for Household wage earners
- ✓ Works with wage earners to develop short-, mid- and long-term goals
- ✓ Ultimately counsels wage earners into and through their personal Household Corporation Spin-Off

Whether you elect to staff each of these positions or not is entirely up to you, provided you are the Head Honcho, of course. Establishing who is in charge of each of these essential functions, however, will help to eliminate confusion among household members, prevent Officers from undermining one another's authority, and put in place the beginnings of your Household Corporation hierarchy, also known as the Pecking Order.

The Pecking Order

"Rank does not confer privilege or give power. It imposes responsibility."
— Peter F. Drucker, Management Consultant and Author

In every business, there is a hierarchy, and it is typically outlined in the form of an organizational chart, which clearly outlines who reports to whom and ultimately who is in charge. While the officers hold positions at the top of the Household Corporation food chain, in any household with more than one person, the pecking order is typically unwritten and therefore it is often assumed that whoever is the oldest among those present is in charge. In creating a streamlined household, the establishment of a written hierarchy is not essential, but putting one in place can certainly put to rest a number of arguments before they ever have the opportunity to occur.

Your Household Corporation organization chart may be broad or general. For the Smith Household – two parents, two kids and a dog – the hierarchy looks simply like this:

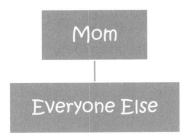

Ready to Launch

In this Household, Dad is the sole breadwinner and feels that the flow of the Household is best left under the direction of Mom, as they agree she best understands the scope of everything that needs to get done over the course of a day, week or longer periods of time, because she is there every day.

As a result of stating that she is most definitely in charge, Mom's decision is never disputed and is always the final word. There is no pecking order among the kids; each is simply assigned tasks and are expected to complete them in the timeframe Mom lays out. The Smiths receive a weekly wage for participating in the duties of the Household and understand what is expected of them. When Mom and Dad are out for an evening, the older sibling is "in charge" which generally means little more than her reminding the younger sibling that it is bedtime as she is already headed off to bed.

Sounds idyllic, right? In truth, it is for the most part, unless you take into consideration typical teenage angst and drama and the ever-present sibling rivalry.

Clear expectations are set for each individual, there is a set schedule (laundry on Tuesday, Thursday and Saturday) and an order for all tasks (first dust, then vacuum). If a project needs to get done, such as heavy yardwork, building a fence or painting the house, it is all hands on deck, working the project to completion in the most efficient manner possible. The reward for a job well-done may simply be dinner together as a family.

As we learned in writing this book and through talking with hundreds of people about their responsibilities and the teamwork and attitudes of their various siblings (or lack thereof), we found that while households with an organized structure like the Smith's often do run more efficiently than most, they are growing less and less common, chiefly due to hectic schedules and the necessity for multiple breadwinners to fund Household expenses.

The experience of most folks, we discovered, is generally far less structured, if there is any structure at all. In attempting to lay out the Jones Household hierarchy, based on our research, we realized that we had to walk through the undirected evolution of the development of a hierarchy.

Ready to Launch

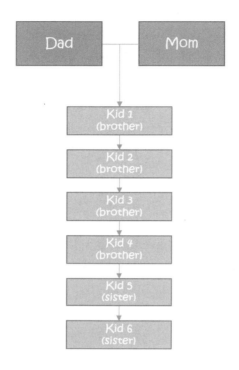

At the outset of its existence, the Jones Household family hierarchy above is pretty straightforward and typical, despite its somewhat unusually large size. The parents reign supreme in the household, followed by the oldest brother, then five younger siblings, in order of age. Mom and dad pass jobs into the ranks and each sibling has oversight over the collective of younger kids.

The Jones family hierarchy begins to diverge from the Smith family when the parents get divorced and remarry, and from there, they undergo a number of organic changes. After the divorce, two households emerge and as we found to be quite common, neither parent wants to be perceived as the "mean" one, so each parent becomes reluctant to hand out undesirable jobs or harsh punishments. Responsibilities that can be delegated to the kids, as a result, are generally unassigned or handed off randomly at best, leaving the kids to determine who is stuck with whatever job is being delegated.

As often happens in a divorce or simply when a kid reaches the teen years, in the Jones Household, trouble emerges, in this case, in the form of oldest brother. His priorities shift to hanging out with his friends and seeking out opportunities to disagree with various authority figures both within and outside the home; he takes on less and less at home and instead turns rebellious and refuses to contribute to any Household effort.

When this happens, younger siblings often turn to the next in line as their natural leader. Regardless of whether that kid is only twelve years old, he ascends to the throne and the order of normal family chaos is restored under his new rule, with the new kid in charge of seeing to it that everyone is fed, makes it to the school bus on time, and gets their homework done. This person is often also responsible for the coordination of travel between parents' homes. Throughout this time, provided the new kid in charge does not seek to wield power for power's sake, great camaraderie among siblings may develop and some may become extremely close, often looking up to one another, as well as even seeing one another as friends.

While it is often assumed among the ranks of the siblings in these types of households that each kid in the pecking order will ultimately have their shot as the lead dog – generally following the line of birth order – we found this is not always the case.

In some cases, and in fact more often than we originally believed would be the case, when the kid in charge moves out (perhaps to head off to college), things do not always go as planned for the next in line. We found several incidences of one kid effectively usurping the anticipated reign of the next in line, resulting in considerable resentment on the part of the skipped kid.

This generally occurs when another kid is wanting to take charge and is ultimately more able to command the respect of the remaining siblings. What we learned happens in this situation, is not simply the development of resentment on the part of the skipped kid, but that individual still perceives they are rightfully in charge, and as such, they develop an offshoot hierarchy based upon their own idea of how things should be. This leads to a very confusing hierarchy, and one which does not generally sit well with the balance of the siblings:

Setting Up the Household Corporation

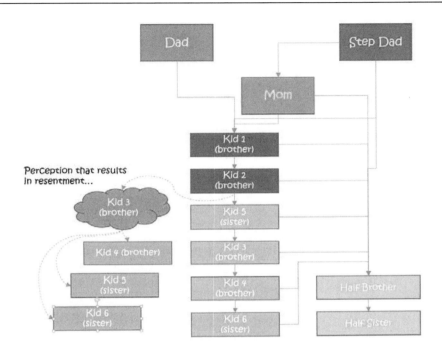

Were any of the Jones parents to intervene and establish a set chain of command for all of the kids, there may be considerably less confusion, possibly less resentment (the kids can simply blame management for poor decision-making and collectively commiserate), and doing so may actually lead to the development of a more team-oriented mindset among all the kids with fewer power struggles.

Of course there is no way to determine or guarantee whether this actually changes the family dynamic, but it is something worth considering, particularly given the increasing commonality of blended families where multiple preexisting spoken and unspoken hierarchies are in place prior to the combination of households.

Regardless of how you elect to set up the formal written hierarchy of your Household Corporation, this is an exercise worth your time. The sooner everyone knows who is in charge and who may delegate tasks and provide supervision and oversight over whom, the more smoothly things may run, especially if everyone knows, helped devise and then buys into the Household Vision.

Vision Statement

> *"The best teamwork comes from men who are working independently toward one goal in unison."*
> – James Cash Penney, JC Penney Founder and CEO

Every corporation, business or household, for that matter, should have a vision – an idea of the future and of where it is headed – before or shortly after the first person comes on board. When creating a service or manufacturing business, that vision may be readily defined by the industry in which it operates or the product which it manufactures (i.e., "we build widgets, and our vision is to build the best and the most widgets and to see that everyone who needs a widget is using our widget"). Defining the vision for a household may pose more of a challenge. Reasons this may pose a challenge might range from a simple disagreement between roommates or spouses or any other member of the household on how things should operate, to something more complex, like the failure to define clear-cut goals for the future.

Ideally, the time for those discussions comes prior to the establishment of the household; however, more often than not, life tends to move forward, regardless of whether a proper plan has been defined. Whether the plan was predetermined or not is now water under the bridge, and from this point forward, it is a good idea to develop a vision for your Household Corporation, which may look something like this:

> *As members of the **Smith Household Corporation**, our vision is to focus on the streamlined operation of the household. In our commitment to that vision, we work collectively to achieve a healthy lifestyle, an accommodating schedule, an agreed-upon level of cleanliness and organization, and an otherwise fairly harmonious existence.*

At first blush, this may seem to be a bit silly, but we assure you, it is not. Your Household Corporation Vision Statement should be developed collectively, and then printed and posted somewhere prominent, where each participating member of the household will routinely see it.

Once you have developed a Vision Statement for the Household Corporation, you will need to determine the jobs and responsibilities that go into the pursuit of that vision; this falls under the jurisdiction of duties held by the Director. By way of example, we are going to break down the Smith Household Corporation Vision Statement into its key components and discuss what this might look like from a responsibility perspective.

The Smiths are seeking to achieve a healthy lifestyle. In their joint discussions on and in the creation of their Vision Statement, to them, this means they would like to eat better – to make healthier food choices and to create a meal plan that the entire household can enjoy. It also means that they are looking to optimize their free time to enable the pursuit of enjoyable activities, and that they want to get sufficient rest (as in the case of the Smiths, sacrifice of sleep and free time in order to keep pace with their hectic household schedule has been a very big ongoing problem).

The second component to the Smith Household Vision Statement is the creation and maintenance of an accommodating schedule. This came about because the kids in this household are particularly active and involved in both community and school activities, but have not yet reached the age or ability to drive. As there is only one car associated with the Smith Household, this is a source of numerous arguments as to whose schedule should take precedence on any given day for any given activity.

The third part of the Smith Vision Statement refers to an agreed-upon level of cleanliness and organization. If this seems to hint at the idea that the kids had any say in the expected level of cleanliness and organization of the Household, it should be clarified that that is not the case. The parents in the Smith Household prefer a clean and organized home, and while the kids prefer that the house is clean as well, they had not previously been committed to keeping it clean and organized and, as such, one parent was carrying the bulk of that responsibility.

Lastly, the Smith Vision Statement closes with the somewhat vague notion of a "fairly harmonious existence." Regardless of the source of the underlying issue, the Smiths, prior to the development of their vision, had experienced an ongoing series of bad days that turned into bad weeks and then bad months, and eventually it seemed they were headed towards a bad year. In sitting down to discuss their vision for the Household, a veritable bickering session ensued, wherein much blame was placed on hormones, lack of sleep, too much homework, not enough free or alone time, and so on, until it seemed that harmony and happiness at home was all but unattainable. However, identifying the problems noted allowed them to work the idea of a harmonious existence into their vision.

While creating their Vision Statement in no way puts an end to fluctuating hormones or occasions resulting in bickering, by posting the Statement prominently, it serves as a reminder to everyone to stay conscious of the family's goal of relative harmony. Further, since the goals outlined in the Vision Statement were arrived at through joint discussion, all members of the Smith Household are more likely to buy into those goals and therefore seek to achieve them.

The Jones Household has a somewhat more complex structure with a far greater number of individuals; however, their Vision Statement is not significantly different from that of the Smiths.

> *As members of the **Jones Household Corporation**, our vision is to focus on reducing the chaos levels of the household and to control the costs of daily living. In our commitment to that vision, we work together to ensure everyone is fed, has clean clothes, has some downtime and privacy, and that no one thinks they are in charge of everyone else.*

As stated previously, there are many more family members in the Jones Household, as compared to the Smith Household. As such, their focus is slightly different, given that they share limited space and resources out of necessity. They seek cooperation and teamwork, and outline their priorities in order to avoid the situations that have historically caused chaos in the household.

While the Smiths have agreed that they want a clean, organized, fair and peaceful household, the Jones family has noted specific priorities, which include ensuring everyone is fed and clothed, and that in the hustle and bustle of their crowded household, everyone has the opportunity for time spent alone. Note that the Jones family has revisited their pecking order, clarifying that no one should feel they are in charge of anyone else; this serves to reinforce what they have already outlined in their organizational chart. Their vision of reducing chaos and controlling costs of daily living serves to foster a spirit of cooperation and thoughtful usage of household items and food. They may choose to further outline their specific cost-controlling measures, which may range from switching off lights when leaving a room to ensuring that all leftovers are eaten in a timely manner to avoid wasting food.

When executed thoughtfully, with the participation of all household members, a Vision Statement clarifies what everyone is working for and towards. It may also serve to clear the household air of various grievances and unfair treatment or behavior. Be prepared to listen and to ensure that each household member is given an opportunity to speak their mind, or the Vision Statement will fail to represent the decisions and goals of the household as a whole.

Section 2
The Job

"Opportunity is missed by most people because it is dressed in overalls and looks like work."

– Thomas Edison, Inventor and Businessman

The Job

Once the Household Corporation is established, the Head Honcho is put in place, the Pecking Order is defined, and the Vision Statement is determined, it is time to figure out what needs to get done. While some Household Corporations will have unique jobs and job descriptions – a few of which we have taken the liberty of outlining in the Appendix, just for fun – most will have a certain set of standard jobs in common that involve things like dishes, cooking, laundry, shopping and yardwork. Please keep in mind that the job descriptions we have provided are simply guidelines; your household may only have one or two available workers, and as such, you may not have any need or desire to create ten separate jobs and so your job descriptions may be far more exhaustive than those presented here.

Regardless of how many separate positions you intend to create, determining which jobs are posted for your Household Corporation requires a little prep work on the part of the officer or officers of the Corporation. Outlining every task that is done (or needs doing) in the Household may initially seem like a daunting job, but frontloading the corporate infrastructure is essential and worth the time it will take to do so. We suggest doing this whether you run a ten-person Household Corporation, or it is just you, as this creates the framework for developing better time management skills.

In addition to the jobs that will be posted, it is important to outline the baseline duties for which each wage earner is responsible and for which no pay is received (for instance, you do not get paid for showing up to work on time, but it is expected that you will). These duties are expected to be done by all who are of earning age – an age determined by the Director – and while earners are not paid for them, they will be included in the periodic performance review. What you establish as the baseline duties for your Household Corporation is a personal choice; however, some of those may include:

- ✓ Making beds
- ✓ Putting laundry away in a timely manner (i.e., within 24 hours of receipt)
- ✓ Clearing dishes to kitchen counter
- ✓ Joint efforts in taking out the garbage (this should not be a paid job)

The Job

Along with meeting expectations for baseline work, it is important that wage earners take pride in their personal appearance. Part of that is proper hygiene and self-care, which includes showering, brushing teeth, using deodorant, getting dressed and so on.

As noted in the Head Honcho section previously, in addition to setting the responsibilities for each job, timing, scheduling, and transportation also become very important. Determining which days of the week are most appropriate for given tasks, based upon the flow of events (i.e., family parties, dinner time, etc.), extracurricular activities and other commitments will be an essential component of setting the proper expectation for any given job.

If, for instance, band practice is always on Tuesday nights, and it is crucial that your resident drummer have a clean band uniform for that activity, it is unlikely that Monday evening is going to be the appropriate night to schedule laundry for this particular Household. Likewise, if the grocery manager is not yet a licensed driver and the only day transportation is going to be available to that manager is Saturday, it would stand to reason that Saturday is the day the grocery shopping needs to be completed.

There will be some leeway, of course, for less schedule-reliant tasks, like cleaning the bathroom, but it should be noted that the individual who holds the job of cleaning the bathroom should not be permitted to, say, prevent his older sister from showering before Prom, just because it happens to be bathroom cleaning day and she failed to mention that she would need a shower.

The Job Descriptions

One of the most important things to keep in mind when designing a job description is the need to break each job down into individual tasks. If the job description is too general (i.e., responsible for the laundry), the job may seem overwhelming to younger kids or overly simplified to older ones. A better idea is to list out the jobs associated with being "responsible for the laundry," writing instead:

SMITH HOUSEHOLD CORPORATION – JOB OPENING
LAUNDRY MANAGER

The Laundry Manager reports to the Director of the Household and works jointly with the Meal Planning Assistant in devising shopping lists. The candidate who accepts this job will earn a wage of $_____ per week, and the job duties associated with this position are as follows:

- ✓ Designating weekly laundry days
- ✓ Gathering laundry from all household members

- ✓ Establishing a method for household members to communicate the presence of stains that require treating or any special instructions (i.e., hang the item to dry)
- ✓ Sorting laundry as required for proper care and by wash temperature
- ✓ Washing and drying laundry*
- ✓ Folding and/or hanging laundry
- ✓ Delivering laundry to household members (Laundry Manager is not responsible for putting laundry away for household members)

Additional duties may include:

- ✓ Maintaining sufficient inventory of laundry supplies and reporting needs to Meal Planning Assistant for inclusion in the weekly shopping list
- ✓ Ironing, as required
- ✓ Laundry Manager may utilize Priority Request Forms (included in the Appendix) to determine order to launder

The candidate who accepts this position must be capable of determining the proper care for all laundry items and must hang items to dry as noted by household members; this position requires a high level of responsibility

This particular job consists of a number of different jobs, and should initially be apprenticed in order to ensure that the person taking on the job will retain the existing Household standards for laundry. There are parts of the job that may even be taught to younger kids and the Laundry Manager might choose to share their wage with a younger sibling in order to have an assistant. This teaches kids not only about managing a staff, but also that the Household Corporation has a set annual budget and in order to hire help for any given job, financial sacrifices might be required.

Open job postings should be found in a household common area (i.e., around the water cooler or perhaps on the side of the refrigerator, in the event there is no water cooler around which your wage earners can congregate for break-time discussions of the overbearing nature of management), where all potential family wage earners can see what jobs are presently available.

Management should provide equal opportunity among potential wage earners for gainful employment; however, the Director reserves the right to set minimum requirements for consideration for employment, which may be based on qualifying events, such as attaining a certain age or maintaining a certain grade point average.

The Laundry Manager description is fairly simple, but touches on all aspects of the positon, including the necessity that the qualified candidate understand the high level of responsibility associated with the position. We have left the wage rate blank, as we will get into that later. If you have the time, energy and desire to do so, you may expand on the description as shown below, which is a posting for the Jones Household position of Kitchen Maintenance I:

Jones Household Corporation – Job Opening
Kitchen Maintenance I

The individual selected for this position will be responsible for the cleanliness of the kitchen and dining room areas as well as ensuring all required supplies to complete the job are kept in stock.

Primary Responsibilities

- ✓ Wash all dirty dishes and promptly put them away, with the exception of any required pre-soaking or scrubbing of pots and pans, as needed
- ✓ Keep the kitchen sink empty of dirty dishes to ensure it can be used when the Executive Chef is preparing meals
- ✓ Clean and disinfect all surfaces in the kitchen area
- ✓ Sweep and mop kitchen floors on a weekly basis
- ✓ Communicate supply needs to the Meal Planning Assistant to ensure that they are purchased prior to running out
- ✓ Clean kitchen or dining room table before and/or after a meal
- ✓ Monitor the refrigerator on an ongoing basis to ensure any spoiled food is discarded and containers are washed
- ✓ Clean the refrigerator on a weekly basis or as needed
- ✓ Ensure all kitchen appliances are clean, inside and out, and in working order (i.e. microwave, oven, toaster oven, dishwasher)

Requirements

- ✓ Overall commitment to cleanliness
- ✓ Attention to detail
- ✓ Timeliness in completing tasks to avoid the unpleasant results of stuck or rotting food
- ✓ Ability to effectively communicate with others
- ✓ Ability to function within a loud and sometimes chaotic work environment
- ✓ Willingness to get dirty on the job

Career Path

- ✓ Upon gaining sufficient understanding of the cleaning process, this individual will be afforded special consideration in taking on the additional responsibility of Bathroom Maintenance I, or any other cleaning position
- ✓ Successful development of a cleaning standard and protocol may permit this individual the opportunity to supervise other Household cleaning staff

Compensation

- ✓ Base wage of $_____, to be paid twice monthly
- ✓ Bonus opportunities will be determined based upon the extracurricular activities and interests of the individual hired for this position

* Time required for this position will vary as the needs of the household change; the successful candidate will outline plans for effective time management in the interview process

---

You will note in the Jones Household, the compensation structure includes bonus opportunities for outstanding work. The Jones family believes in incentivizing wage earners based on the individual interests of each new hire and works to identify and explore those opportunities in the interview process.

In addition, the Director of the Jones Household has included a career path that may serve to incentivize a wage earner to continue taking on new responsibilities and thereby earning more money.

On a side note, if the Director determines that an earner is not fulfilling the duties of their position to the required standard, he may elect to confidentially notify other household earners of the opportunity to gain that position (vis-à-vis a confidential job posting). All wage earners should be made aware that this policy exists and no job should be offered without providing the job holder a performance review and the opportunity for remedial training prior to losing the position.

If you elect to approach your wage earners with a proposal of this sort, you should take the time to stress the importance of confidentiality and discretion, as this will prove to be a valuable skill once in the actual workforce. It should be further noted that it is not an opportunity to taunt, tease or otherwise disparage a fellow wage earner. This will allow competitive earners the opportunity to take on more responsibility and may serve to motivate kids to hold themselves to the highest standard of work for that position.

Wages

wage

/wāj/

noun

1. *A fixed regular payment, typically paid on a daily or weekly basis, made by an employer to an employee, especially to a manual or unskilled worker.*

In our long discussions with respect to compensation, we struggled with different approaches to paying wage earners for their efforts, and the long and the short result of our efforts are this – there is no single, perfect or completely fair way to structure salaries. We were able to agree, however, that age should not be a determining factor when considering the wage associated with any given job.

In theory, an older kid will take less time to do a simple job (i.e., emptying the dishwasher) than would a younger, smaller kid who may need a stepstool to put various items away. The older kid is not being penalized for being older, but rather incentivized to take on more responsibility as a way to increase their overall wage. As the desire for increased income becomes a primary focus, discussions should move to time management strategies and perhaps taking on a more pivotal role within the Household Corporation. Increasing the salary of a given job based solely upon the age of the wage earner creates a system that penalizes younger individuals for not being born sooner.

When setting wages for any job, we agreed that several factors should be considered in every case:

1. *What is affordable for the Household Corporation.* Wages need to be paid in a timely manner and as such, they should be set first, based upon the ability to routinely meet the wage earner salaries at the intervals set by the Financial Officer; this will tie directly into the Household Corporation's annual operating budget.

2. *How frequently wages are going to be paid.* If the Household Corporation is capitalized (Director gets paid) twice per month, then keep that fact in mind when setting the timing of wages paid – if it will be difficult to meet *weekly* payouts due to the timing of income to the Household, then the payouts to wage earners should be set accordingly. Not only will this benefit the Household for ease in meeting those commitments, but will also provide wage earners with a reliable, set pay schedule, which will allow them to learn the basics and benefits of budgeting.

3. *What is a realistic rate of pay.* This is really important. Even if your Household Corporation has considerable discretionary income to share with your wage earners, it is absolutely imperative that wages are not set too high for any given job. Not only does this stand to create a potentially unrealistic expectation for wages once the kid heads out into the real world, but it may also prevent your young wage earner from looking for work outside the home. If, for instance, the kid is earning $100 every two weeks for taking out the garbage and doing the laundry (even if it does include his

sister's band uniform), he may not have any interest in an $8.25/hour first job.

4. *How much time does it take to do the job.* Taking out the garbage and doing laundry are quick jobs that require little real time commitment. To earn a comparable bi-weekly wage from a job paying minimum wage would require a time commitment of at least 7 hours per week, when taxes are taken into account. As such, the time spent on a job should certainly be factored into the wage set for that job.

If the wage is set appropriately, it will be based not only upon the time associated with completing the job, but also everything that goes into preparing for and cleaning up after the job. In the case of lawn maintenance, not only is the wage earner responsible for the job (including edging, mowing, sweeping up afterwards, taking bags to the dump and so on), but she may need to plan around uncontrollable factors like the weather (e.g., the right day to fertilize or treat for pests based on predicted rainfall) and will also need to factor in time to shower afterwards, particularly if mowing needs to be done in 90°+ heat.

5. *Who is counting on the job getting done.* In addition to the time commitment expected to complete any given job, the level of responsibility and reliance of others on a successful job outcome should also be considered and priced into the wage. Getting everyone's laundry done in a timely manner is far more of a

concern than whether someone has vacuumed beneath the couch cushions, for instance.

6. *Who wants the job.* The expected popularity (read: **demand**) of the job should also play a factor in setting the wage, as some jobs are less likely to produce an interview inquiry, based solely on how icky they are to complete. Conversely, if everyone is willing to do the job, the wage can be lowered to encourage those capable of taking on more responsibility to actually do so.

Jobs that are less desirable and therefore potentially worthy of a higher wage, or a wage *Premium*, may include those with an associated:

a. **Fear Factor.** This describes any level of intimidation that a wage earner may associate with a given job. Cleaning the gutters on a two-story house is much more dangerous than doing the laundry while standing on the ground, for instance, and as such the demand for the gutter cleaning job may be lower than that of the laundry manager, resulting in a Fear Premium baked into the wage of the gutter cleaning job.

b. **Ick Factor.** This refers to the inherent unpleasant or unsanitary nature of a particular job. There may be less candidates willing to take the job of cleaning the litterbox, as compared to the candidates willing to empty and reload the dishwasher, which should result in an Ick Premium being associated with the litterbox job.

The Job

c. **Minutiae Factor.** This is characterized by the monotony or tediousness of a particular task. While this job may not be particularly difficult, if it requires doing the same task over and over again, it may affect the desirability of a particular job. By way of example, dusting is not a particularly difficult job, nor is it widely noticed. Having to move every item in the house in order to dust under it, especially when done regularly, is decidedly boring and not as visually rewarding as mowing the lawn, where the results are obvious to everyone. A Minutiae Premium may be used in order to generate interest in this type of job.

d. **Intellectual Factor.** If a job requires critical thinking skills, qualified applicants may be in short supply; this may include jobs that involve managing the family finances or coordinating workable transportation schedules for all household members. An Intellectual Premium should be paid for jobs that require exercising the gray matter.

e. **Cautionary Factor.** Washing all of the glass swans on the knick-knack shelf requires greater care than sweeping the floor, for instance, as failure to exercise caution might result in the snapping of a little swan's neck, putting the wage earner's own neck at risk. If a job requires extra care and patience, a Cautionary Premium may be added to the wage.

f. **Responsibility Factor.** This underlines the importance of a particular task and the reliance of others on it being completed. For instance, all household members rely on the Laundry

Manager to ensure that their laundry is clean, and as such the Laundry Manager is taking on more responsibly than the person in charge of dusting the house, since failing to dust on time does not directly affect the household members. A Responsibility Premium should definitely be assigned to positions where others are counting on the job being completed on time and with the expected level of care.

Once the jobs have been determined, descriptions have all been written (or copied straight out of our appendix), wages have been set and the schedule for the completion of those jobs is at least roughly outlined, it is time to rally the team for the first Staff Meeting to discuss the rollout of the Household Corporation. In this meeting, a ceremonious display may be made of posting the Household Corporation Vision Statement, or everyone may simply be informed that jobs will be posted within 24 hours and all interested candidates should plan to submit their resumes for consideration.

In a Household Corporation with only one potential wage earner, the Director should still post all jobs for which they could ultimately be eligible (even if they are outside the current abilities of the earner), so that the employee can see which jobs lay ahead. The solo wage earner can then develop the time management skills necessary in order to take on more responsibility as a means to increase their wage by taking on additional jobs.

Resume, Please

This chapter is geared towards kids developing what is most likely their *first* resume; however, the fundamental principles can certainly apply to anyone engaged in the somewhat arduous process of determining what they like, what they are good at, what experience they have that applies to the thing they like, and then organizing all that information succinctly into a one-page dissertation on their personal excellence. There is an entire section dedicated to writing a well-polished resume later in this book.

Kids should be encouraged to take on the task of creating their own first resume. Doing so will help them gain an understanding of the critical thinking that goes into designing one, and may lead to not only a better understanding of their own skills and talents and how best to market them, but possibly better long-term job prospects over time. Of course, when designing a career-oriented or professional resume, the focus is generally placed on outlining duties performed at jobs once held by the person writing the resume. Clearly, if an 8-year old is writing a resume to apply for a job posted on the refrigerator, it is unlikely they will have a long job history to flesh out the *experience* section – which is why the process of writing this initial resume is one that requires focus, attention and a little creative thinking.

When looking for a job as an adult, it is routine to seek out those positions for which one knows they are already qualified and then to prepare a one-page summary of every place they have previously done the tasks required for the job to which they are applying. We suggest starting out differently (and not just for kids). By going through the steps that follow, we hope all readers – whether building their first resume, or their latest – gain a clearer understanding of what needs to be in that document – both explicitly as well as implied.

Start by determining the job you *want*. Note that we did not suggest to start with the job *for which you are already qualified*. Kids should thoughtfully and thoroughly review the job postings, giving consideration to the time, energy and effort that goes into each position. They should also consider the types of experience they will gain from each posted position and how that may apply to their job prospects going forward, whether within the Household or external to it. By focusing on the end result (i.e., "one day I intend to be the Household Corporation Financial Officer" or "one day I intend to start a thriving lemonade stand"), they will be more likely to structure their job evolution based on the skills they need to acquire through experience in order to obtain that position.

Next, review the job and determine what *underlying* skills are required. If we take the position of Laundry Manager outlined earlier and lay out the duties associated with it, they look like this:

- ✓ Designating weekly laundry days
- ✓ Gathering laundry from all household members

- ✓ Establishing a method for household members to communicate the presence of stains that require treating or any special instructions (i.e., hang the item to dry)
- ✓ Sorting laundry as required for proper care and by wash temperature
- ✓ Washing and drying laundry
- ✓ Folding and/or hanging laundry
- ✓ Delivering laundry to household members (Laundry Manager is not responsible for putting laundry away for household members)

While the potential candidate for this job may never have done any of the duties listed, that does not indicate whether that individual is qualified for the job. In fact, with proper training in each process, mastery of the duties is possible, provided the interest in attaining that mastery is there. The resume submitted for this job should reflect that interest as well as the applicant's ability to learn quickly and to take on responsibility. Consider that the resume-writing process is really simply expressing an understanding of the candidate's strengths on a more conceptual level, given, in this case, their unproven (i.e., nonexistent) track record.

Skills to list on the candidate's resume applying for this job might include:

- ✓ Demonstrated attention to detail, as evidenced by accuracy in math homework and ability to proofread own writing

- ✓ Outstanding scheduling and time management skills, as reflected in commitment to extracurricular and volunteer schedule on top of academic load
- ✓ Strong desire to contribute to the flow of the household in support of the Vision Statement by virtue of applying for a job which requires mastery of not only scheduling, but the use of equipment and meeting the needs of each individual in the Household Corporation
- ✓ Interest in developing leadership and problem-solving skills for future endeavors; have always enjoyed solving puzzles, brainteasers and playing video games

While it may seem odd to add in the note about playing video games, consideration should be given to the skills which video games may actually help kids develop, such as:

- ✓ Ability to think quickly and make decisions
- ✓ Multi-tasking
- ✓ Quick reflexes
- ✓ Problem solving and big picture strategizing
- ✓ Teamwork and communication (in certain multi-player games)
- ✓ Resource management
- ✓ A desire to win and achieve – something which seems to be fading in the *everyone should get a trophy for participating* world of non-competitive, gentler sports and activities

This is the type of outside-the-box thinking that should go into the construction of a resume, whether you are a first-timer or have held several professional positions. Everyone develops a skillset over the course of time, regardless of whether those skills (and the applicability thereof) are easy to discern initially. Learning the process of any given job is generally not insurmountable, when proper training is provided and a desire to succeed exists.

Now, it is now time to put pen to paper, or if your potential candidate is computer-savvy, they may elect to type their resume instead. Formatting the initial resume does not need to be labored over, but it should be neat and cover some key points. The level of formality is up to the candidate, but when it comes time for interviews, potential wage earners should be made aware that they may be in direct competition with other applicants, and therefore may wish to put their best foot forward.

Section 6, *Writing the Real Deal Resume,* goes into extensive detail with respect to crafting a professional-looking resume. We suggest sharing that section with your potential wage earners when they embark on the task of writing their resume.

The Interview Process

Depending upon the size of your Household Corporation and the number of available wage earners seeking any given position, you may offer interviews for more popular positions, or even for all posted positions, regardless of popularity or number of interested candidates. Interviewing is essential, and a skill that will be used throughout your wager earner's life.

In keeping with this mindset, deadlines should be set for each job posting (i.e., two weeks from the date of the posting). In the timeframe between the posting of the job notice and the deadline, potential wage earners should be encouraged to submit their resume and a cover letter for consideration for the position. Once the deadline has been reached, interviews should be scheduled and conducted. At the establishment of the Corporation, this may prove to be a long process, given the number of tasks being divided up; however, once the positions are filled, interviews will only need to be conducted for vacancies, which may occur due to poor performance, outside business activities or employment opportunities, or even a Corporate Spin-Off.

In the interest of fairness, the Director of the Household should conduct all initial interviews, which should be scheduled in fairly short order following the deadline for applications. This will prevent favoritism to some degree and will ensure that all qualified applicants are afforded similar earning opportunities as well as the same amount of time to develop their resume. *Why even go through this process?*, you might ask – the simple answer is this: while you may have the ideal candidate in mind for a given position, that does not mean that another candidate should not be afforded the opportunity to persuade you that they are, in fact, a better candidate for the position.

The interview process should be conducted with true sincerity, should you wish for the candidates to take the process seriously. Since many Directors may have only been on the receiving end of the interview process in their career (and therefore perhaps having blocked out the stressful and painful memories of various questions asked in those interviews), following are some thoughtful questions you might pose to the interviewee, along with the reasoning behind asking them. Of course, if this is a formality because there is only one potential wage earner in your Household Corporation, you may choose to ask entirely different questions.

1. *Why did you choose to apply for this position over the others that were posted?* Determining what motivates your young wage earner will provide you excellent information for their personnel file, so if the response is that they picked the job because the listed wage was the highest, you learn that they are motivated by money. If, on the other hand, they express they are interested in the level of responsibility associated with the job, you learn that they are perhaps motivated by a desire to be of as much help as possible. If they choose the job because it is the only one with which they have no experience, then they are likely motivated by an ongoing desire to learn. Understanding what motivates your kid will help you develop an incentive and reward system that will work more

effectively for them. For instance, if your wage earner is compelled to learn at all times, they may prefer a gift certificate to a book store over the cash bonus sought after by the one who is money-focused.

2. *How do you feel this job will prepare you for your future?* While your applicant may ask you for clarity as to what you are looking for, you should refrain from guiding them to a response, as how they interpret the question is equally important as their answer. If the response is that they intend to learn how to do laundry (or whatever the job is for which they are applying), then they are likely very practical and are likely not looking much beyond what lies immediately before them. If instead they respond that they feel this will help them work in a team environment and support the betterment of the Household Vision Statement, then you know you have a more long-term strategist on your hands. They may also say they have no idea how this will apply to or prepare them for their future. Regardless of how the applicant responds, this is an opportunity to engage in a thoughtful conversation with respect to thinking about how what is done in the present has a direct effect on the future. It should also be pointed out that developing longer-term goals may help them determine which skills they may seek to acquire from their initial and subsequent jobs. This may also be a good time to remind them of the exercise they engaged in while crafting their resume and suggesting that they think forward to what this the proposed position will add to their skillset, like management experience, financial experience, or process development.

3. *What is the minimum wage you would accept for doing this job?* If the response is that they expect the posted wage, then their understanding is that you have considered what the wage *should be* for the given task and therefore that is what they expect to receive. If, instead, the response is that they are willing to work for free, so long as they earn the respect of their siblings and can learn the job as posted (admittedly, this is an unlikely response once the applicant is approaching the teen years), then you learn they do not assign a specific dollar value to their time or their efforts. Regardless of the response, we do not feel this information should be used to reduce overall wages paid, but rather to provide you with a framework for their initial performance review. If the candidate said they would perform the job in the absence of pay and then does brilliantly on the job, it is likely that they already have an extremely strong work ethic. Those who come in below expectations may need additional training, discipline and encouragement to foster the same ethic.

4. *How do you feel you are more qualified than the other candidates for this position?* If the applicant launches into a discourse on how they have always sought to help out in the house, that they take on responsibility willingly and have excellent follow-through and reliability, you learn that they have a clear idea of their own strengths and that they are looking to build on them. On the other hand, the applicant may take this opportunity to shift the focus of the interview to why the other candidates are less qualified than they are (i.e., Jimmy is lazy and only wants to play video games). This type of response may indicate that the applicant is more

concerned with their performance relative to others, rather than focusing on their own abilities and accomplishments. Relative performance focus often has a detrimental effect on morale overall, as well as the collective Household productivity, as those who are given to this type of thinking generally seek to further bring down those around them in order to elevate themselves. This provides an opportunity to remind all applicants that reviews are done individually, based solely on each individual's merits and performance, and that seeking to damage the confidence or character of others is frowned upon and will not be tolerated.

5. *How will you seek to improve the quality or speed of the job?* Brainstorming various ways to improve job performance, prior to even starting the job, will provide you with some valuable insight as to the candidate's critical thinking skills, as well as their desire to master the task. This may change how they view their on-the-job training, as they may be looking for ways to increase the quality of their work, while simultaneously seeking out ways to become more efficient and lessen their time spent with each task they are taught.

6. *How do you feel your performance of this job will serve to further the Household Vision?* The response to this question will help determine whether the candidate is aware of the Vision of the Household Corporation and whether they take it seriously.

7. *Do you have any questions about the position or the Household Corporation?* Candidates may take this time to impress you with

how deeply they have considered the position and what goes into the job; they may have a number of technical questions or they may have no questions at all. If they have considerable technical questions, you may assuage any potential fears by assuring them that in the event they are hired for the position, they will be given full and proper training on the job and that further questions may best be saved for that time. If the questions surround the pay rate, the benefits, the time commitment, or whether or not all the associated duties are actually essential to the position, these may serve as warning signs that the candidate is already looking to slack on the job.

Additional questions may center on the candidate's personal strengths and weaknesses, where they see themselves within the next year, or any other question the Director feels applies to the given position. Questions should be consistent for each candidate however, again in the interest of fairness to all applicants.

We strongly suggest taking notes through the interview process and retaining those notes in a file designated for each wage earner. These notes will prove helpful when it comes time to complete initial and subsequent performance reviews, as well as in setting future goals.

Once all the candidates have been interviewed for any given position, thoughtful consideration should be given to whom you consider most appropriate for each role. While one candidate may be older or appear to have more knowledge, equal opportunity should be afforded to younger candidates so they do not become discouraged by always losing out to their older sibling. Fairness in hiring practices goes a long way towards collective Household morale, and leads to far less commiseration over the short-sightedness of management.

The Job Offer

Now that you have your candidate in mind, it is time to send a formal offer. The job offer should be a written letter that outlines for the candidate at least the title of the position, the rate of pay, the frequency of pay, the term of the job (some will be seasonal, while some are annual and ongoing), and any benefits being offered. A job description for each job being offered should also be included with the offer letter so the duties of the proposed positions are made entirely clear at the outset. A sample letter follows below:

April 1, 2016

Warren Jones
123 Homefront Drive
Ourtown, ST   98765

RE: Job Offer with Jone$ Inc.

Dear Warren,

Ready to Launch

The Jones Household is pleased to offer you a job as Laundry Manager. We trust that your dedication to the outstanding personal appearance of all members of the Household will be a valuable asset to the continued harmony of our Corporation. Should you choose to accept this job offer, we would like you to begin your apprenticeship and transition into the role Friday, April 8th. With proper training and skill optimization, this is position requires approximately four (4) hours per week. Per Corporate policy, you will be eligible to receive the following wage, benefits, and bonus opportunities beginning on your hire date.

- Starting Pay: *Salary of $4.00 per week*
- Pay Period: *Every other week (on alternating Fridays)*
- Job Term: *Ongoing, with quarterly performance assessments*
- Benefits: *Household match of 25% to qualified savings plan*
  Vesting schedule for access to Household contribution
  One week vacation
  Two personal and/or sick days
- ✓ Bonus Opportunities: *Opportunities for bonuses are only offered to earners in good standing with the Household Corporation who are routinely completing the duties of their position to the highest level of quality and in the timeliest of manners; upon successful completion of a three-month training and probationary performance review period, you will become eligible for the following possible bonuses:*
    - *Mini-golf with one guest*
    - *Invite a friend to sleep over*

By signing the acceptance of the job offer outlined above and in the attached Job Description, you are acknowledging that you will be accepting a high level of responsibility with the Household Corporation and participating directly in the pursuit of our collective household goals.

To **accept** this job offer:
    Sign/date this letter here: _____ _____

To **decline** this job offer:
    Sign/date this letter here: _____ _____

The Job

The Jones Household hopes that you will accept this job offer and looks forward to your contributions to the smooth and harmonious operation of the household. Should you have any questions or concerns, please reach out to Pops Jones directly.

Sincerely,

Pops Jones
Corporate Director, Jone$ Inc.

If the candidate accepts the offer, retain a signed copy of the offer letter into their file, and schedule their on-the-job training. If, however, the candidate should decline the offer, put a signed copy into the file and extend the offer to the next most-qualified candidate. This may come in handy in the future should the individual who turned down the offer question the fairness of management in its offer process; it should be evidenced that they were afforded equal opportunity and declined the offer. If the candidate is willing to say why they opted not to take the job (i.e., the pay was lower than expected, it seemed like too large of a time commitment, etc.), make a note on the letter prior to filing it. This may again help in future interviews as well as performance reviews, as this may reflect a pattern of laziness, a lack of teamwork, or a skewed view of the financial value of their work.

What to do About Unclaimed Job Postings...

Every so often, or perhaps more often than not, there will exist a job that nobody wants to take on (i.e., emptying the litter box, pulling weeds, etc.), and these may be difficult positions to fill. That said, those jobs still need to be completed.

> *I once had a candidate come in for a job interview who had started his illustrious career cleaning up vomit from the grass at the state fair – think tilt-a-whirl-and-hurl... He spent six years at that job, and after that number of years on the job, and with a commitment to his own personal growth in the job and his future success on his mind, he made his way up to managing a staff of his own. The question I posed to him was, after that many years in service to the job, and in light of the fact that he now oversaw a staff of his own – who cleaned up the vomit? His reply was, "if there was vomit on the grass and I was available, I still cleaned up the vomit." This statement alone is why I hired this particular young man, and why he's the coauthor of this book. This simple comment, in conjunction with the fact that he had remained on such a job for six consecutive summers, showed me that regardless of the monotony (or indeed the disgusting nature) of any given job, he was a loyal and hardworking person committed to the greater good. Even if that greater good equated solely to the removal of vomit from the grassy arena of a state fair ground.*

The Job

Your Household Corporation may or may not have a candidate willing to serve the greater good, but again, those jobs still need to be completed. Likewise, if you have interviewed candidates for various positions and they have declined the formal job offer, this may leave an unclaimed job hanging in the balance.

Based upon the amount of time required to do any given unclaimed job, the Director may have to resort to utilizing using negative incentives to compel everyone to pitch in.

First things first, reoffer the job. This time, however, the original wage should be prominently crossed off in red pen with the new wage reflecting only half of the original wage (i.e., $2/week for the Laundry Manager versus the original $4). Reposting of the job should be performed ceremoniously with everyone present, if possible. You may elect to make an announcement that no one has claimed a given position and now it is being reoffered at half the original wage.

This will likely generate confusion among the members of the household, who may immediately raise the point that if no one was willing to do the laundry for $4 per week, why would anyone do it for $2? This is an excellent question and creates an opportunity upon which you should capitalize. Whether as the closing to a glorious speech centered on the collectively-designed Vision Statement reiterating the importance of teamwork and the goal of family harmony, or just in a simple statement, you may choose to say that since no one was willing to accept the responsibility at $4, management has elected to give everyone a chance to receive $2 for doing so; however, should no one choose to take the job for

$2, the entire household will all take on the responsibility collectively, in rotation, *without pay*.

Once the looks of consternation and disbelief fade, someone will either step up to the plate to claim the $2 per week stipend, or it will be time to map out the schedule to train the entire household in the process of the unclaimed position and to assign each person, in rotation (we suggest alphabetically, rather than by age), their day of responsibility for all the tasks associated with the job. To be clear, the job should not be broken down into individual tasks and divvied out among family members, but rather each individual will be held to the household standard for *all* the work associated with the job on their day in rotation.

If someone accepts the job at $2, however reluctantly, you may choose to then restore their positive incentive stating that following a one-month probationary period under quality supervision, they may become eligible for a restoration of the original $4 per week wage.

While there are several possible options that may incentivize all household members to pitch in, our only suggestion is that you never ***increase*** the wage associated with a given job in order to draw in applicants. Not only might this push your household beyond its budgeted dollars for any given time period, but it will also result in your wage earners realizing that if they just hold out long enough, a higher wage will be offered. Accepting that a given job is being offered at a given rate is something that is likely to come up repeatedly over the course of a lifetime, and this may help young wage earners develop a sense of capitalizing on opportunity when it first comes knocking.

First Day on the Job: Orientation

One of the more common mistakes made in training young wage earners is in failing to provide a complete picture of the responsibilities and duties that go into any given job. The task of cleaning the bathroom may mean one thing to you and a completely different thing to that wage earner, and as a result, the execution of the job may fall short of your expectations. As such, take orientation and training seriously if you want the job done well, as you can only hold the wage earner to the standard you established in the first place, and if you failed to fully outline the duties of the job, they cannot be expected to know what they are doing or even why, in many cases. Consider the following true anecdote by way of example:

"My first attempt at gainful employment occurred at the age of nine, when I applied for a job in Oscar Swanson's neighborhood grocery store. I was hired on the spot and was pleased to begin my career in the grocery trade, at 10 cents an hour. All in all, not bad for an inexperienced juvenile in 1947! With minimal orientation, I was assigned duties as a stock-boy with the responsibility of keeping the shelves full and the fresh produce prominently displayed. Eventually, I was called upon to assist in check-out operations as a bagger. Within a few weeks, I was again called upon – this time to assume the important role of Egg Candler and, while it may appear that I was being "fast-tracked" up the ranks, this is in fact where my career took a rather nasty turn.

Ready to Launch

In the back room of the store, I was set up at a table, opposite a steel bucket, placed upside down over an illuminated light bulb. The bucket had two holes cut into it, each slightly smaller than the diameter of a typical hen's egg, that the allowed the light to shine through. To the left of the bucket were several stacks of large crates, each containing God knows how many eggs, purchased from local farmers; and, to the right sat a stack of retail-sized cartons into which "candled" eggs were to be placed and then stocked for sale. On my first daunting day at this important job, I was told that the process of candling eggs involved placing each individual egg over one of the illuminated holes in the bucket, followed by arranging twelve of the candled eggs into each of the cartons to be stocked and sold in the store. Mr. Swanson must have assumed I already possessed a greater knowledge of candling, due perhaps to having been born in the great state of Iowa, as no further explanation was offered and my training and orientation were complete. As a thoughtful young man, I assumed that the heat, the light, or a combination of both, did something to render the eggs suitable for sale, and that seemed sufficient knowledge to me, at least, for an Egg Candler.

As it turned out, there was in fact no magic involved and I shortly learned that the purpose of shining that light through each egg was to determine whether the egg contained spots of blood or other unpleasant surprises, thereby allowing Mr. Swanson to avoid what occurred within a day or two, when a group of rather angry customers returned quite a large number of my carefully candled eggs…

Perhaps as a reward for my outstanding performance as an Egg Candler, I was immediately moved out the back door of the store and across the alley to a space Mr. Swanson maintained for bulk potatoes, where my new job duty was to sort the good potatoes from the rotten ones. While it turns out I was far more skilled at sorting than candling, after one day in the rotten potato bin, I elected to leave the grocery trade altogether and pursue my dreams in the entertainment industry, starting out as a pin-setter in the local bowling alley." – Dwight J Lucia

While Dwight may have been quite capable of learning the egg-candling process, Mr. Swanson failed to provide him with sufficient information to understand the job – not only what he was doing (that the candle did not somehow magically render the egg edible), but why (to look for blood spots in eggs and then toss those eggs) and the ramifications for failure in completing the job to specifications (angry customers complaining to management about the quality of the products offered at the grocery store). All three components are essential when providing training:

- ✓ What the tasks are and how to complete them
- ✓ Why they are to be completed in this way
- ✓ What may happen if they are not

In the interest of giving a clear example on how to do this process, let's break down the job of cleaning the bathroom for the Smith Household. Below is the job description for the position and what follows is one manner in which training might be offered to the wage earner who secures the position within your household:

SMITH HOUSEHOLD CORPORATION – JOB OPENING
BATHROOM MAINTENANCE LEVEL I

It is the job of the Bathroom Maintenance Level I worker to provide for a clean and healthy bathroom environment for those utilizing the facilities. The bathroom(s) under the jurisdiction of this individual should be cleaned and sanitized in the manner outlined below one time per week, on a set day as outlined and agreed to by management.

Job Duties

Specific broad duties for the job of Bathroom Maintenance Level I include:

- ✓ Cleaning mirrors
- ✓ Disinfecting and scouring shower/bathtub
- ✓ Disinfecting and scouring vanity top and sink
- ✓ Disinfecting and scouring toilet – inclusive of the bowl, under the rim, the seat, the lid, the tank and the base
- ✓ Scrubbing the floors
- ✓ Washing light fixtures
- ✓ Removing used towels to laundry (based upon the schedule as determined by Laundry Manager)
- ✓ Washing towel rods, toilet paper roll holder, knobs, fixtures
- ✓ Keeping Management informed of needed cleaning supplies

Training Protocol

It should be noted that it is expected by Management that the bathroom(s) covered under this job description will be fully cleaned in one cleaning session. If multiple bathrooms are included with this job, they may be cleaned on different days of the week, based upon mutual decision with Management or as set out by the wage earner, provided the individual has been granted decision-making authority.

Training the wage earner hired for this position should be executed in the form of an apprenticeship, alongside and at the direction of the individual currently performing the duties up to the Household standard. If the role is being assumed by a wage earner for the first time, the training should come from the Director or other qualified officer. If the role is being passed down after an older wage earner secures work outside the home or is headed off to college, that individual should apprentice the young wage earner. If, on the other hand, the job has been offered for availability due to poor execution, the individual in the current role should not be called upon to train the new hire, and the apprenticeship should return to the responsibility of the Director or other qualified officer.

Regardless of who provides the training, it should be done so in a descriptive, demonstrative, and incredibly thorough manner – as though the new hire has never performed any form of job duty previously. By training in this way, rather than by basing it upon the new hire's implied understanding of the job and required skillset, the trainer will ensure that no details are missed, all tasks are done to specification, and thus will significantly improve the likelihood of success of the wage earner, ideally resulting in better initial performance reviews. A positive initial review may serve to boost the confidence of the wage earner, resulting in the possibility of a stronger work ethic and bolstered commitment to the Household Corporation.

In the case of the Smith Household Bathroom Maintenance Level I position, training should include at least the following:

- ✓ An overview of supplies to be used for the job; such as:
  - Rubber gloves, which should be used in order to avoid injury while cleaning with water at the hottest possible temperature in order to boost the effectiveness of the cleaning supplies as well as to increase sanitizing effect.
  - The proper type of sponge (if fixtures are ceramic or stainless steel, the Director may specifically not allow the use of abrasive sponges).
  - A cloth, towel or paper towel for drying surfaces (the Director may find paper towels, while convenient, to be wasteful and expensive and prefer that a retired cotton t-shirt be used in their place).
  - Cleaning products – not every young wage earner will know, right out of the gate, the difference between window cleaner, multi-surface cleaner, shower cleaner, toilet cleaner and so on; to them, it may all be blue and therefore able to be utilized on any surface. If the Director prefers specific cleaners be utilized for specific tasks, that should be explicitly taught, both verbally, as well as by example. An explanation of the differences between cleaners may also prove helpful. If the Director prefers that only all-natural

cleaners be used, the reasoning for doing so should also be taught.

- Any equipment which may be utilized, such as the toilet wand, vacuum, mop, shower squeegee, or other equipment as deemed helpful by the trainer. When introducing equipment, the trainer should provide a detailed lesson in how to properly operate and maintain the equipment (i.e., if the vacuum canister is full, the wage earner will need to know how to empty it). Extra attention should be paid to explaining the necessity of keeping equipment with electrical cords away from water to avoid electric shock. Keeping equipment clean and sanitized is essential in this role as well.

✓ The predetermined Household method for performing each associated task, including at least the following:

- Explaining that household cleaners should not be sprayed on and then immediately wiped off; they should be sprayed onto a surface, allowed to work for a period of time and then scrubbed or wiped away.

- In addition to washing the floors and fixtures, all should be completely dried prior to exiting the bathroom – this may help prevent slipping or other possible hazards that might come from wet floors or other surfaces.

✓ The most efficient order in which to complete tasks and the rationale behind doing so – washing floors as the final task makes more sense than doing it first, given the need to stand on that same floor while cleaning everything else – which might look like this:

- First, remove all items from each surface to be cleaned – as oftentimes items found in the shower are wet on the bottom, additional care should be used to ensure that they are not set anywhere that might be damaged; placing a used towel (that will ultimately be gathered for the laundry manager) onto the floor provides a reasonably safe spot
- Next, spray the mirrors with glass cleaner
- While the glass cleaner goes to work, spray down the vanity counter, the toilet tank, lid, seat and base and set aside
- Add toilet cleaner to toilet bowl, ensuring to coat the bowl from the water level to the ring
- Using a dry cloth, wipe the mirrors clean, ensuring no streaks are left behind
- Run hot water into the vanity sink and use to scrub down all sprayed surfaces; the same cloth used for the mirrors may be used to wipe those surfaces dry and to wipe clean the light fixtures as well as the towel rods, door knob or other fixtures
- Using the toilet wand, scrub the entire toilet bowl; toilet cleaner should not be left stuck to the sides of the bowl; wipe the toilet dry in its entirety so as not to leave a wet seat or slippery surface
- Once all surfaces are clean and dry, the floor should be scrubbed, one section at a time, starting at the deepest corner of the room, backing out towards the door to avoid having to step across a freshly-washed, likely wet floor

- After the floor has dried, items should be returned to the shower and to the countertops, wiping off the tops of each prior to putting them in their designated places

By properly outlining everything that is expected and the reasoning behind why things are done the way they are, the wage earner understands the fundamentals. Once those have been understood and mastered, the wage earner (and indeed all wage earners in all positions) should be encouraged to seek out more efficient or creative ways to accomplish tasks, while still maintaining at least the same standards, in order to save time and personally expended energy.

Effective Time Management

> *"I choose a lazy person to do a hard job. Because a lazy person will find an easy way to do it."*
> – often attributed to Bill Gates

Time management is an important, yet elusive, concept in life, not only to young children and teens but often just as equally to adults. The most common complaint we hear from kids is that there is not enough time to get everything done. We get the same complaint from the adults we coach, so this is not a generational issue. The key components to effectively managing time at any age include: organization, understanding the scope of the task at hand (and how many underlying tasks constitute the main task), allotment of sufficient time to complete any given task, structuring time positively, and most importantly, the elimination of procrastination.

From there, time management begins and ends with knowing and understanding everything you *want* to do as well as everything you *have* to do. Time, managed effectively, can feel as if it lasts much longer than a mere 60 seconds per minute. Outside of their jobs, most people waste more time watching other people do nothing than they themselves spend doing something. If you don't believe this fact, consider that the average person watches around five hours of television per day. Per day. That's not five hours with a football game on for background noise – that is five hours of sitting. Or 300 minutes *per day* that could be filled with literally any other activity.

We firmly believe that nothing is all that time-consuming, provided you understand what goes into completing any given task. You then simply streamline each component of the process, based on the most time-efficient way to get it done with the best quality and the least amount of expended energy.

> *"Nothing is particularly hard, if you divide it into small jobs."*
> – Henry Ford, Entrepreneur and Inventor

Consider an experiment one of us ran with regards to making coffee. In and of itself, this is a very simple job and one that is not particularly time consuming to begin with. The coffee pot in this particular kitchen is situated beneath a cabinet, like this:

Ready to Launch

the coffee was up here

four inches of clearance here

As shown in the picture, the coffee is housed in the cabinet above the coffee pot, while the coffee filters are in a different cabinet altogether. When pulling the coffee pot out away from the wall in order to fill the water reservoir, the lid must be lifted, which obscures the ability to open the cabinet to remove the coffee. Originally, the pot was pulled away from the wall, the reservoir lid was lifted, the previously used coffee filter and its contents were tossed in the trash while the water pitcher was being filled in the sink, and the lid was then closed so the coffee could be removed from the cabinet. By simply moving the coffee to the same cabinet where the filters are kept, which is *not* situated above the coffee pot, fifteen seconds of work and extraneous movement (including opening and closing the reservoir lid twice, rather than a single time, and opening two cabinets rather than one) was eliminated.

While fifteen seconds may not sound like much, in terms of free time, it should be noted that each minute contains those sixty seconds to which we referred earlier. Saving fifteen of them conserves a full quarter of the minute. Done effectively over the course of each minute of an eight hour work day, this process can conceivably restore two full hours of productivity, or free time, to your day. While not every task can be distilled down in this way, once you begin looking at the individual components of each task you complete, you may begin to see ways to cut down on wasted effort, just like the lazy person Bill Gates would hire.

The largest contributor to poor time management is, of course, procrastination. When given the option of working on things now or doing so later, most people will opt for later – this is particularly prevalent in kids with respect to homework, but often equally so with adults on the job. The inherent underlying issue in putting everything off until later, however, is that eventually later arrives and everything you have saved is sitting there in a pile, smelling like last week's laundry, and you no longer have sufficient time in which to complete everything, because now you have those tasks slated for today on that same pile. Given that comparison, let's consider what procrastination looks like in the Laundry Manager position...

While the tasks encompassing the job of Laundry Manager are not particularly time-consuming or difficult (i.e., gathering laundry, sorting laundry), one thing that cannot be changed or streamlined is the amount of time it takes to wash or dry a load of laundry. On top of that, if an article of clothing must be laid flat or hung up to dry, rather than being tossed into the dryer, considerably more time is going to be required in order to fully complete the job. So in this case, when *later* arrives, not only will all the laundry that was put off until later need to be done, but so will all the laundry that will have built up in the meantime – something perhaps the

Laundry Manager has neglected to consider. So whereas, on a typical wash/dry day, there might be three loads of laundry, in this hypothetical scenario, there are now six loads of laundry, but only sufficient time after a full day of school, to complete the usual three.

To get the job complete, the Laundry Manager will now likely overload the washer, shorten the wash cycle, dry something that should have been hung or laid flat, and possibly deliver a shrunken, damp band uniform to a sibling. A resourceful Laundry Manager bent on doing a good job might seek out the assistance of the Household Transportation Coordinator in order to gain a ride to a laundromat; however, that will require loading the car, securing the time of the Transportation Coordinator (which, if this person is thinking, should come at a price of some magnitude), and obtaining sufficient quarters to complete all the laundry in tow.

Not only is procrastination widely endemic, it is also a hard lesson that is seemingly learned in perpetuity. Commenting on procrastination generally results in an exaggerated eye roll and an "I know, I know" response, and yet rarely seems to change, regardless of the age, gender or business acumen of the individual rolling their eyes.

In the interest of developing a strategy to minimize (notice, we did not say *stop*) procrastination, we suggest starting with the following:

1. Make a list of everything that needs to get done; this can take any of several forms – either in a to-do list, on notecards with one task per card (helpful for ongoing, repetitive tasks, like the components of the laundry process), or on a computer spreadsheet, whichever works best for you.

2. Set a due date/time for completion of each task; there may be long-term tasks that you have no intention of completing immediately included in your task list.

3. Determine the amount of time required to complete each task or component of each task; you may do this in your head or you may write it out next to the item. Writing it down initially may prove helpful, as it is generally the case that we initially *underestimate* the amount of time it takes to fully complete a task. Adjusting the time allotted to any given task will be beneficial going forward in better helping plan out your time.

4. If certain tasks have associated prerequisites (i.e., in order to dry the laundry, it must first be washed), then the order should be noted.

5. There may be tasks which can only be completed at certain times and on certain days (i.e., transportation to the grocery store, participation in football practice, etc.); make a note of that fact next to the task so that fact does not go unnoticed.

Following is a to-do list with all these factors taken into consideration:

Stuff I have to do

What	Time	When
Shower	10 minutes	Every day
Go to school	7 hours	Monday-Friday
Eat breakfast	15 minutes	Every day
Eat dinner	30 minutes	Every day
Football practice	3 hours	Mon/Wed/Sat
Football games	5 hours	Every other Friday
Homework	Usually an hour	Most days
Clean upstairs bathroom	30 minutes	Tuesdays
Clean basement bathroom	30 minutes	Thursdays
Empty litter box	5 minutes	Every day
Volunteer at animal shelter	4 hours	Saturdays
Read something I like	30 minutes	Every day
Go to bed early		Sundays
Hang out with friends	Don't know	When I can
Play chess with bro	An hour	When we can
Build model car with dad	Forever!	When we can

Once your list is complete, you can move forward with scheduling your time. If you are a young wage earner going through this process, you will have to consider not only those tasks associated with your Household Corporation job duties, but also practice schedules, if applicable, as well as unknown amounts of homework as noted in the sample list above. Social time, downtime, and time to eat should also be figured into planning time effectively, as these often go unnoted and wind up suffering, skipped, or being rushed through as a result. Time blocking may seem unnecessary at first, but it helps develop discipline with respect to managing and saving time, an understanding of the level of responsibility associated with managing a busy schedule, and even the ability to allow time for spontaneity, despite how counterintuitive that may sound.

Starting the day with three quick wins is important – a quick win is anything that can be done in under 15 minutes. Doing so sets you off on the right foot and helps you feel as if you have completed something right away. In the case of the example above, there are only a couple of quick tasks – emptying the litter box, showering and eating breakfast. This is what a week of time-blocking might look like for him:

Ready to Launch

SUN	MON	TUE	WED	THUR	FRI	SAT
	6:30 wake	6:30 wake	6:30 wake	6:30 wake	6:30 wake	6:30 wake
	litter box	litter box	litter box	litter box	litter box	litter box
	shower	shower	shower	shower	shower	shower
	b'fast	b'fast	b'fast	b'fast	b'fast	b'fast
	7:30 bus	7:30 bus	7:30 bus	7:30 bus	7:30 bus	
	read	read	read	read	read	
7:45 wake	7:45	7:45	7:45	7:45	7:45	7:45
	school	school	school	school	school	football practice
litter box						
shower						
b'fast						
8:30 free time						
						11:30 animal shelter
hang with friends or work on car with dad	2:45 bus	2:45 bus	2:45 bus	2:45 bus	2:45 bus	
	read	read	read	read	read	
	3:00 home	3:00 home	3:00 home	3:00 home	3:00 home	
	3:15 homework	3:15 homework	3:15 homework	3:15 homework	3:15 homework	
						3:30 read
	4:30 dinner	4:30 upstairs bathroom	4:30 dinner	4:30 basement bathroom	4:30 dinner	4:30 chess
5:30 dinner	5:30 football practice	5:30 dinner	5:30 football practice	5:30 dinner	5:30 football game	5:30 dinner
6:00 free time		6:00 free time		6:00 free time		6:00 free time
8:30 bed						
	9:00 free time		9:00 free time			
	10:00 bed	10:00 bed	10:00 bed	10:00 bed		10:00 bed
					11:00 bed	

When blocking time, it is important to factor in travel time, as well as a buffer of 5-15 minutes around larger activities that may run past the allotted time. This will help alleviate stress associated with managing a packed schedule to the extent possible. If you find yourself stuck in

The Job

traffic but have allowed for those extra several minutes, it will not seem as if your day has gone off the rails and you will be able to recover the flow of your day as time passes.

You will note in the example that this young man elects to do the bulk of his leisure reading on the school bus. This is a wise use of time; while he may not feel that the environment is appropriate for doing homework, he chooses to use this time to do something he enjoys while traveling. Free time is scheduled in, in addition to time he has already set aside to play chess, work on the model car with his dad, and to hang out with his friends. If he is disciplined and conscientious, he will find that even with an extremely busy schedule, he has sufficient time for additional unplanned activities that he might also enjoy. He has even considered the necessity of sufficient sleep and has planned for an early, restorative night on Sundays as he knows he will need to be ready to go first thing Monday morning, all the way up to and including a very strenuous three-hour football practice after dinner.

Once this method has been employed for a period of time – for at least several months – scheduling tasks and events and extracurricular activities is more likely to become second nature, and may ultimately not require such a strict adherence to the process. This is simply one way to develop time management skills which will be used throughout life, and which may ultimately be a cornerstone of a strong resume and exemplary work ethic.

Section 3

Running the Corporation

"Start with good people, lay out the rules, communicate with your employees, motivate them and reward them. If you do all those things effectively, you can't miss."

– Lee Iacocca, American Automobile Executive

Once the jobs have all been posted and filled and the Household Corporation falls into a functional day-to-day rhythm, there are several points of consideration for keeping things running smoothly. You will want to ensure that every member of the Household is performing up to the expected standard, that discipline is being administered as necessary at appropriate and fair levels, that there is ample opportunity to air grievances, and that methods are in place for keeping morale high in what may be, at times, a fairly stressful and fast-paced work environment. The Household Corporation will always be evolving and keeping these key points in mind, as well as offering opportunity for professional and personal growth are essential to a well-run organization.

Reviews

First things first: reviews are required. It cannot be expected that a young, inexperienced wage earner will just inherently know whether they are doing a good or poor job. Anyone who has ever been in the workforce without a formal review will likely attest to the fact that not hearing how they are performing creates a detachment to the position. In a review scenario, consider whether the wage earner is performing (for this example) at or below their expected level of work... by not hearing from Management that they are failing to meet the basic expectations of their position, they are operating under the assumption that the work they are doing is sufficient. On the other hand, if a wage earner consistently goes above and beyond the call of duty, putting in extra effort and even taking on perhaps more than initially outlined as per their job description, and it goes unacknowledged, that wage earner's motivation may decline. In the case where both of the wage earners outlined are members of the same Household Corporation and neither gets a review and both continue to receive full pay and benefits, the message being sent is clear: doing the bare minimum is sufficient and going above and beyond will not be rewarded.

> *"It is no use saying, 'we are doing our best.' You have got to succeed in doing what is necessary."*
> – Winston Churchill, British Prime Minister

Consider the life and career of a professional athlete…

Let's say you're the coach of Serena Williams and you are responsible for her professional growth and development of her athletic skillset. Chances are, you are going to want to comment on her swing more than once per year, as failing to comment in real time would prevent her from seizing the opportunity to make adjustments to her swing before the bad habits became permanent.

Having and maintaining a great workforce is as much about effective management as it is about the workers. If you are paying attention to the performance of your individual wage earners and taking time to make note of exemplary behavior as well as "strikes" against any individual with respect to their job performance, you will be better prepared to provide a thorough assessment of the job performance of that wage earner. General references to "doing a good job" will have little impact, as opposed to saying "when you clean the mirrors, I notice that you take the time to ensure there are no streaks left behind – that is excellent work." Being specific matters.

How often to review… Let's go back to Serena. Remember how we said she needed more feedback than one ten-minute session once a year? Imagine you are now erring on the side of overcorrection (or as it is more commonly known in the workplace: micromanagement) – in this scenario, you are correcting every swing, commenting on every step, making adjustments each time she makes a play. This is far too much feedback, and may only serve to create insecurity in your wage earner, instilling in them the sense that no matter what they do or how they do it, they will never receive a positive or encouraging word from management.

Reviews should be conducted quarterly in the first year of the wage earner's employment with the Household Corporation, and on a similar schedule whenever new job duties are being assumed, as it is wise to make corrections prior to an incorrect process becoming engrained. Once the wage earner is in a stable position and things are going smoothly, you may choose to reduce reviews to a bi-annual or annual schedule.

Review commentary, at whatever interval it comes, should be constructive, positive and encouraging. If criticism needs to be levied, it should be done so gently and with purpose and should not feel insulting or belittling to the recipient.

It should additionally be noted that reviews are not the appropriate time to take in feedback regarding other Household members, and instead should remain focused on the performance and personal experience of the individual being reviewed. If there is some misunderstanding of the scope of the job being performed however, or successful completion of the outlined job is predicated upon the performance of another person (i.e., the personal responsible for grocery shopping failed to purchase the supplies necessary to complete the laundry), then those issues may certainly be addressed during the review.

Reviews should be conducted as an open conversation, starting with how well the wage earner feels they are doing on the job, whether or not they feel they have mastered their job, what they have done to streamline any procedures (if applicable), and whether they have satisfaction in the work they are doing. Further discussion can include any difficulties they are experiencing and what they feel they are learning through their work. After the reviewee has been given the opportunity to go into detail in this regard, the Director should provide an equivalent amount of feedback on their performance, their attitude, and their contribution to the overall operation of the Household. Employee Evaluation and Employee Self-Evaluation forms are included in the Appendix to give you a starting point for conducting an effective review.

As a last point in this section, keep in mind that utilizing anecdotes, fables, stories and even metaphors is an excellent way to impart meaningful philosophy during a review about the importance of a strong work ethic, good time management or fiscal responsibility, as in the personal example that follows:

Grandpa K. would always tell the story of two lumberjacks. One lumberjack is a big burly Paul Bunyan-type of guy, while the other is a wiry little guy cutting logs bigger than his thighs. The little guy challenges the big guy to a log-splitting competition and the Paul Bunyan guy is more than happy to oblige, and incidentally, laughs his way through his acceptance of the "challenge," knowing full well he can best the little guy with very little effort. The day comes for the competition and both show up, axes in hand, each facing felled trees by the dozen. They get to work – the big guy begins splitting logs effortlessly, cutting through logs like a hot knife through butter. The little guy matches his efforts but takes two swings to each single swing of the big guy. Every twenty minutes, the little guy would take a break, grab a glass of water and sharpen his axe, returning to his work with a renewed sense of purpose and continues with his former pace. The big guy just laughs, swinging his axe through the morning. As afternoon closes in, the little guy continues his pattern of taking breaks, staying hydrated and sharpening his axe, sustaining a two-stroke pace per log. At this point, the tables begin to turn as the big guy is becoming tired and his unsharpened axe is requiring two and occasionally three strokes to split each log. His pace slows and his humor starts to wane. As evening falls and the end of the competition approaches, the judge returns to the cutting area to find the little guy chopping logs, two strokes at a time, whistling as he works. The big guy, however, has collapsed from exhaustion, his stunted and dulled axe at his side. The bell signaling the end of the competition is sounded and the tallies are drawn. The little guy, with his determination, pacing, skilled preparation and thoughtful consideration of what it would take to get the job done, wins.

The point my grandpa hoped to get across to me (I started out as a fairly wiry kid) was that if I prepared, hung in there, had a good attitude and did the job the right way, I would persevere and win out in the long run. He used this to show me that it is about more than just strength, size or being born with talent – work ethic, attitude and perseverance can overcome any perceived shortcoming. – Brett Pawelkiewicz

Correction and Discipline

We want to begin this section with a heartfelt apology to all of the potential wage earners who may be subject to the disciplinary actions suggested in this section, which have fallen under the jurisdiction of the writer who is much closer to childhood (or perhaps at least more inclined to understanding and embracing childish behavior) and is therefore addressed from his perspective...

I know that growing up, had my parents known of some of these options, I would have been much more cautious before doing anything that would have caused me to be punished. I had the benefit of growing up during a time when being grounded and ultimately sent to your room was much more of a reward than a punishment, as it meant that I would be able to watch television or play video games uninterrupted. My parents had believed they were subjecting me to solitary confinement; however, as keeping track of my various electronics proved difficult for them, I quickly learned that headphones allowed me to feign arduous, silent suffering. One of the main reasons I laid claim to writing this section is due to this gap in knowledge between what a parent may still view as a punishment versus what today's kid considers punishment.

With that out of the way, I would like to directly address those reading this and those who may be implementing the disciplinary measures detailed out below. As I thoughtfully considered and detailed out the punishments I knew I would have hated as a child, I felt a bit of a Benedict Arnold, giving away the secrets of my own people, so bearing that in mind, I want to express sincerely that many of the punishments listed below should not be employed unless under the direst of circumstances. While a red-painted back porch will hurt less and less by the hour, some of the punishments I am proposing will last much longer than that and therefore are likely to carry with them considerable bitterness and grudge-holding from the recipient.

When considering taking disciplinary measures, careful thought should be given to ensure that the punishment suits the crime. Yelling in a public restroom, for instance, should not carry the same weight as shaving a sibling's head while they sleep. So bearing that in mind, I offer forth the following, which suggested levels of punishment:

Running the Corporation

Light

1. Unpaid work – assignment of a job or portion of a job for a set period of time (i.e., one week) to be completed without pay; failure to meet the quality standards of the job throughout the duration of the punishment may result in a week-long extension.

2. Grounding – this old-fashioned punishment is a classic, but difficult to enforce effectively in this age of electronics. The offending party should be sequestered to a room without a television or any other entertainment option, such as the dining room, in the interest of ensuring the designated room is free from all potential electronics. The individual's cell phone should also be confiscated at the outset of the punishment and all siblings should be instructed to avoid the Grounding Room. If the offending party is found with electronic contraband, a warden can be assigned to oversee the punishment and receive the offending party's wage for the day.

3. Snack ban – while this started as simply a restriction of dessert following dinner, that seemed a little light to even be considered a

light punishment, so we elected to expand the restriction to all snack items (i.e., chips, crackers, candy, gum, pudding, etc.) for a set period of time.

I promise I won't do it again!

Medium

1. Actual face time – restricting time with phones has become a modern-day classic, and while this may require a refresher course in verbal communication for the offending party, the eye contact alone may prove to be a solid punishment, particularly for teenagers. This can be customized to suit many differing levels of punishment from a light punishment of a couple hours to a medium or heavy punishment of multiple days.

2. Cancel that – if a sleepover, trip to the movies or even just hanging out at the mall is already scheduled amongst the offending party and their friends, cancel the event entirely.

3. Sidelining – while the severity rating on this punishment may vary with the offending party's interest level in their activity, missing a practice, game, concert, rehearsal or other scheduled extracurricular interest or activity may serve as a solid punishment. Of course if their grade depends upon their attendance, we would advise against missing the concert or game.

High

1. Back to the bus – once your wage earner has acquired the sweet reward of the freedom that comes with having a driver's license, removal of access to a vehicle (particularly for driving themselves to school, as this means a return to the bus) will seem cruel and unusual to them, which is exactly the idea behind this type of punishment. Any errands, dates or outings will require arrangement of alternate transportation.

2. Distraction contraction – like the forced unplugging, but this includes the use of any phones, tablets, laptops, televisions or gaming systems (unless electronics are being used solely, and under strict supervision, for completing homework). By removing access to all bright and shiny screens with flashing lights and Las Vegas-style soundtracks, the offending party will be forced to look up and interact, and may come to the realization they "have it pretty good" and then may avoid making the mistake of disobeying upper management in the future.

3. Amending the Permanent Record – this formal write-up must include the details of the misconduct, an explanation from the offender as to why the misconduct occurred, as well as a signed agreement outlining the punishment should this misconduct be repeated in the future. Depending upon the severity of the misconduct, a formal write-up may result in reduced wages, the forfeiture of bonuses or exclusion from corporate events.

That's the last straw...

ULTRA High

1. Working the Chain Gang – this forfeiture of pay can be for the entire wage earning period or for a portion of it, depending on the size of the forfeiture, whether the offense was a repeat occurrence, or whether it resulted in monetary damages.

2. Smartphone Lockdown – lockdown and replace their smartphone with a dunce (flip) phone. Flip phones can be purchased for a relatively small amount of money (about $15), and simply switching out the SIM cards will allow for the dunce phone to be activated. Now the offending party may only use their cell phone for calling/texting and will not be able to post that picture of their dinner on Instagram. This is a fairly visible punishment, as all their friends will see they have been relegated to the Flip Phone Brigade. The length of time this punishment is enforced can vary depending on the nature of the offense.

3. Death by Lethal Deletion – this punishment has been reluctantly included on the list by this particular author. As someone who enjoys playing video games, this punishment would have been devastating had it been used on me. Kids often have numerous hours invested in a particular video game, and simply *threatening* to delete their file might convince them to behave. The complexity of deleting a saved gaming file has only increased with the sophistication of gaming systems, but a simple internet search will reveal step-by-step instructions to do so.

Where correction and discipline are concerned, we feel we should include a few items of note. First, even if your desire is to be the "friend" parent (i.e., non-disciplinary), all kids benefit from discovering where their reign ends and the real world and its rules begin. Second, it is essential to understand that when levying discipline, it may feel more like a punishment to the person providing it than that of the recipient (i.e., *"this is going to hurt you more than it's going to hurt me"*), because it often means listening to whining, complaining, heavy sighing, and so on. And third – this is the most important rule of all – do not threaten a punishment on which you have no intention of following through. If you say you will delete the save files on a video game, for instance, be prepared to back that up with the wherewithal to actually follow through – empty threats (i.e., *"if you don't stop that, I'm going to take all your stuffed animals out into the yard and set them on fire"*) carry little weight and create a lack of respect for the authority of the person in charge of dishing out the discipline.

Regardless of how you elect to instill martial law within your Household Corporation, we recommend that consideration always be given to the appropriateness of the punishment as it relates to the misdeed, and that discipline be delivered in a timely, if not immediate, manner.

Tattletale Box

Having an anonymous, safe and fair way to address issues is essential in order to maintain an equitable work environment, as it ensures that all complaints are addressed in an unbiased manner. Complaints may range from *"Jimmy never paid back his loan,"* to *"when Jimmy misbehaved in the same exact way I did, I got a high level punishment and he only got a light level one."* Addressing these concerns without a screaming match or a "he said, she said" type of argument aids in learning of and correcting any issues as opposed to getting into an emotionally-charged argument where feelings get hurt and the original issue ultimately only takes a back seat to name-calling.

Although creating a safe way to bring genuine complaints or concerns to the attention of management is important, it should be stressed that overuse of the Tattletale Box with petty or frivolous complaints is not acceptable. In the Real World, it is equally important to bring up and air out real issues; however, being labeled as a "tattletale" at any point in life is never seen positively. A person labeled a tattletale may find it difficult to earn the trust of their peers, as their peers may be hesitant to speak their mind if they feel it will be used against them later. As such, acquiring the critical thinking skills necessary to determine whether lodging a complaint is productive is best done early on, prior to the development of bad habits which may negatively impact relationships and job opportunities in the future.

With that in mind, a Tattletale Box may be set up in an area of low traffic so that attention is not brought to anyone depositing a complaint into the box. The box should ideally be lockable, with a slit for a piece of paper to fit into, as this will prevent curious wage earners from seeing whether anyone has lodged a complaint against them, as only the Director will have access to the tattletale box. It should be also said that any complaints regarding the Director need to be kept in strict confidentiality. One snarky comment from the Director along the lines of, *"we have to make sure Warren gets as many carrots as Jimmy, since we wouldn't want anything to be **unfair**."* (looks at Warren), may be intimidating to a wage earner. This may prevent the filing of any future complains out of fear of being ridiculed or called out. Everyone in the Household Corporation should be encouraged to speak their mind without fear of intimidation, bullying, or retaliation for doing so.

In the interest of developing the critical thinking skills to determine the validity of a complaint, we have a list of potential grievances which should **always** be brought to the attention of the Director:

- ✓ Verbal or mental cruelty
- ✓ Physical altercation
- ✓ Theft of or damage to personal property
- ✓ Unfair management practices (i.e., routine favoring of one person over another)
- ✓ Missed job duty

Not every complaint is worth filing. Most people have heard at least once in their lifetime that they should learn to *Pick Their Battles*. The grievances that follow *may or may not* need to be reported and the intention of the filer and the individual being reported should be considered when making the decision to file the complaint:

- ✓ Unauthorized use of property – there is a substantial difference between using a sibling's power cord to charge an electronic device without asking versus absconding with their gaming system, erasing their game settings and then hiding it under the bed afterwards.

- ✓ Invasion of privacy – whether expressly outlined or not, there is typically a level of privacy that is expected in a household; however, entering a shared bedroom to use the bathroom should not be construed as a true invasion. Invasion of privacy complaints are best addressed with a reinforcement of the harmonious household vision and a reminder that simply knocking before entering a room (and then waiting to be acknowledged and given permission to enter) is a sign of mutual respect.

- ✓ Schoolwork issues – where schoolwork is concerned, each household member should hold themselves to their own performance expectations. Grade marks received in school will generally reflect whether homework is getting completed and it is not the responsibility of an individual to report their sibling for not doing their homework. However, if two kids share a room and one is routinely up with the lights on late at night doing homework while the other is trying to sleep, this is a valid complaint and should be reported.

- ✓ Poor job performance – job performance and whether or not it meets the household standard may be somewhat subjective, and as such, consideration should be given to whether a complaint of this nature is valid. If there is a streak on the bathroom mirror following a routine weekly cleaning, it was likely an oversight by the Bathroom Maintenance worker and likely does not need to be reported; however, if the Laundry Manager has not gotten the laundry completed in a time manner (or at all), then complaining is truly warranted.

- ✓ Attitude issues – everyone occasionally has an attitude problem, particularly once the teenage years arrive. This is not to say that attitude problems should not be reported, but rather consideration should be given to the nature of the attitude. A quiet bad mood should not carry the same weight as a screaming match.

As mentioned, the Tattletale Box should not become a repository for every petty sibling argument, but rather seen as a constructive way to clear the air and make note of inequities. This is why strict confidentiality of the contents of the Box must be maintained. It is up to the Director to determine how and when to address the complaint or issue, be that within the framework of a review (if it is performance-based) or immediately upon notification (as in the event of a physical altercation between siblings). The contents of the Tattletale Box may even lead to a restructuring of Household rules, a more creative approach to discipline or simply just a more harmonious Household environment for everyone.

Keeping Morale High

As anyone who has worked a job will likely attest, earning a wage is generally not sufficient in and of itself to keep morale high, but maintaining a collectively positive attitude is hugely important in all firms. Even small incentives go a long way towards creating an enjoyable work environment, which typically lead to happier, more engaged and productive workers who have a vested interest in seeing their firm grow and succeed. Since one of the purposes of this book is to get kids actively engaged and to buy into the betterment of their Household Corporation (read: **family**), what follows are a few ideas for incentives that may prove easy on the pocketbook while also helping to create a fun, healthy work environment. It should be noted that incentives should be treated in much the same way as punishments in that the *coolness* of the incentive should be commensurate with the level of goodness in the good deed. If one wage earner is continuously given treats for doing their job while the other is only given a verbal acknowledgement of "good job," resentments will develop, as will an unfair work environment, which is counterintuitive to keeping morale high.

Collective incentives are those incentives which apply to all wage earners and are intended to be used to not only as a reward, but to additionally bring the family closer together. Some ideas may include:

- ✓ Family movie night – rent a movie, pop up some popcorn the old fashioned way (on the stovetop) and gather everyone together to enjoy a movie. If deciding which movie to watch becomes a problem, rotate through each Household member, draw names from a hat or even draw previously agreed-upon movie selections from that same hat.
- ✓ Whistle while you work – or perhaps more appealing, listen to music. The music selected should be something that everyone will enjoy and can preferably sing to (nothing says family bonding quite like everyone singing Bohemian Rhapsody together at the top of their lungs).
- ✓ Fortify – a few kitchen chairs and an assortment of blankets are more than sufficient to turn a room into a fort George Washington would be proud of. Younger kids can be given the option to sleep in the fort for the night, or everyone can hunker down, crawl in, and watch a few heartwarming kitty videos on the internet together.
- ✓ Ice cream – because who doesn't like ice cream…
- ✓ Family game night – if your teenaged wage earners see this as less of an incentive and more as a punishment, you may wish to reserve it as one! If it is seen as a positive, be sure to rotate through games that are interactive and fun and offer a level of friendly (or deadly serious) competition for everyone.

✓ Breakfast for dinner – while to some this may sound silly, this is often actually a household favorite, and one of the easier, more cost-effective ways to get the family well-fed (and who ever heard of veggies for breakfast anyway??).

Individual Incentives are awarded to a specific wage earner and should be used as recognition, outside of bonus opportunities, when someone goes above and beyond what is expected of them. These may be granted to more than one wage earner in any given time period but the individualized nature of the reward may not make that entirely feasible. Some ideas for these may include:

✓ Stock up on their favorite snack

✓ Permit them control of the main Household television – this may be for playing video games or watching a show; be sure to set a time limit

✓ Host a sleep over – keep in mind that while this reward is fun and exciting to the individual who earned it, it may be quite disruptive to the remainder of the Household, so be sure to set clear ground rules to ensure other wage earners are not pestered while the friend is over (if chaos is embraced, allow everyone a friend over as a collective reward)

✓ Take them out for a fun activity or a meal – this may take the form of one-on-one time with upper management, which is especially valued in larger families where one-on-one time may be much harder to come by

- ✓ Provide quiet time/privacy – while in smaller families this may not be classified as an incentive (as any time can be quiet time), in larger families, quiet time/privacy is often a rare commodity; if this incentive is offered to a wage earner, it should be stressed to any siblings who may share living quarters with the individual that quiet time is being granted and to be certain it actually remains quiet
- ✓ Permit use of the family car – while this is fairly self-explanatory, if there is only one Household vehicle and the scheduling of that vehicle is very tight, this may prove to be a very coveted reward

Whether wage earners are rewarded collectively for showing exemplary commitment to the Household Vision or individually for doing an outstanding job in some respect, making note and providing some form of formal recognition is important. This provides a positive incentive versus simply the risk of correction or discipline that comes with a negatively incentivized work force.

Outside Business Activities

Once your wage earner has learned the amount of work that goes into earning a dollar, and subsequently understands the value of that dollar, they may choose to seek outside employment of some kind. Some kids – those with early entrepreneurial promise, perhaps – may elect to start their own business venture, like a lawn mowing business or perhaps a babysitting service. Launching a small business, even when it is simply offering the neighbors a low-cost option for landscaping, can quickly become a serious venture, and should be treated as such. If your kid is going to take the time to go door-to-door to solicit business, then a conversation built on time management, setting proper expectations, reliability and money management is most definitely in order.

If that seems over the top, consider the following example, where Warren Jones has decided he will start a lemonade stand…

Ready to Launch

Warren is looking to start up a lemonade stand. The Director is willing to take his interest seriously and to honor his desired professional direction. At this point, a meeting of the Officers of the Household Corporation is called, and Warren is invited to attend.

The first order of business will be a joint discussion with respect to setting proper expectations and time management. As it stands, Warren is presently earning a Household wage for his work as Laundry Manager, Kitchen Maintenance I, and as Household IT Manager, and he needs to determine whether he will have sufficient time to continue in those roles while pursuing his new venture. It will need to be reinforced that this is the time to set proper expectations not only for the Director, but also for himself and ultimately his future clientele. It is irresponsible to launch a business venture without first assessing the real commitment required to make it a successful one. Since Warren believes he will be able to continue to meet all his present Household obligations while pursuing his dream of owning and operating a lemonade stand, he should be prepared to support his convictions with a sound time management plan. Warren should be reminded he needs to factor in the time he will spend working on the establishment of his business as well as the time to he needs to actually operate the business – both in peak season as well as in the off season, should there be one.

If, however, Warren believes his new venture will take up the bulk of his time and he will therefore need to resign from his Household roles, some determination will have to be made with respect to coverage of the duties associated with his various Household jobs. Since there are additional siblings (or more accurately, a larger workforce) who are willing to interview for those roles, coverage is likely and Warren's resignation will less likely to disrupt the harmony and overall productivity of the Household Corporation. If Warren was an only child, his resignation may have a more noticeable effect. Consideration should be given to all these factors as well as the additional resources that Warren may need in order to launch and operate his venture.

Next, in the event Warren has provided a sound time management plan and, if warranted, agreed to a short-term apprenticeship of his siblings in order to ensure a smooth transition of his Household roles, it is time to address reliability. While this may not be as essential with a lemonade stand as with a lawn-mowing or babysitting business, being reliable is an important part of any business. Is this a rain-or-shine venture? Is a regular clientele important? Will the stand be moving locations periodically to gain greater market share? Wherever and however the business is run, reliability – even if it is simply the reliability of the quality and cool temperature of the lemonade – is essential, as reliability is the cornerstone of building a good reputation. Working when perhaps you are tired, the weather is poor, or you just do not feel like it are all hallmarks of a strong work ethic, which is perhaps the most valued trait in the Real World.

>*"Discipline is the bridge between goals and accomplishment."*
>
>– Emanuel James Rohn
>American Entrepreneur and Author

Money management, or the finances of the new business venture, is a broad topic and one that should be broken down into multiple components. First comes the idea of funding the venture – or more to the point, where is Warren going to come up with the money to get this off the ground? If Warren has been working for the Household Corporation for a period of time and has saved some or all of his earnings, he may have sufficient capital to enter into his enterprise unfettered by the necessity of seeking startup funding. If Warren does not have the resources, or would prefer not to tap his savings in order to start the business, he may need to find a lender to finance his venture.

In either of these scenarios, Warren should take the time to outline the costs associated with his startup, as that process will provide him with crucial information, such as how much he will need to earn in order to recoup his startup capital or to repay the lender of the funds. Warren considers that while he knows he can simply set up a card table at the end of the driveway, borrow the yellow flowered pitcher in the kitchen, buy some lemons and sugar, and ask for a stack of Dixie cups from the bathroom supply, he would prefer to have a more professional-looking business. It is, in fact, his hope to not only start a business, but to also embody his own philanthropic spirit and donate a portion of his profits to the local animal shelter. He is hoping to build his business, in part, around his cause and therefore would like his stand to reflect his purpose.

First, he finds a design similar to his desired stand:

Ready to Launch

He then makes a list of items he needs to build and operate the stand in order to project his estimated start-up costs:

Stuff I need:	
Wood planks (need 3 pallets - $5 each)	$15
4'x4' posts for sides (need two - $7 each)	$14
Paint (ask for samples at the home center store)	FREE!!
A picture frame (to show shelter animal of the week)	$3
Cooler (for ice)	$2
My own pitcher (I want a nice one that isn't plastic)	$10
$10 in singles to make change	$10
Lemons (two bags)	$10
Sugar (five pound bag)	$3
40 5-ounce clear plastic cups (2 bags of 20)	$5
My total to start this:	$72
Once it takes off, I will need:	
Wheels for the stand	???
A way to hook it to my bike	???
To pay Jimmy to work with me	???

Running the Corporation

After making his list, Warren realizes that although he has saved enough money to start up the venture, his account is not fully vested and as such, he will seek to borrow the money from the Household Corporation. The Director is willing to lend him the startup money to get the venture off the ground, provided he writes a sound business plan and then shows how the business will be sufficiently profitable to pay back the business startup loan. This step can provide incredible insight into the business process.

Items addressed in the business plan may include the following:

Determine how and when you will be profitable:

- ✓ Based on the yield of your lemonade recipe (i.e., one half gallon), calculate the amount of each ingredient that will go into your lemonade for a set amount of product (i.e., the proposed glass pitcher, which is one *full* gallon).
- ✓ Calculate the current cost of each *ingredient* per batch of lemonade and, using that data, calculate the total cost per batch.
- ✓ Determine how much will equal a serving and how many servings can be derived from each batch.
- ✓ Divide the total cost per batch by the number of servings to calculate the cost per serving. This is the product base cost and does not take into consideration the cost of labor and time (shopping, production, setting up the stand, marketing, etc.), nor does it take into account any profits. This is incredibly important, because the startup loan will be repaid with the profits. Net profits, minus the cost to fund the next batch, go to the Household

Ready to Launch

Corporation until the loan is paid back, after which those profits can be kept or shared with the animal shelter.

✓ As a second exercise, consider what will happen to the cost of production and the resulting profits should the cost of lemons increase by, say, 3%, or if the cost of sugar should decrease by $0.05 per five-pound bag. How will those price changes affect the way business is run? Will prices need to be raised? Will the tried-and-true recipe need to be altered? Will profits decline? How likely is it that either of these scenarios will occur? Remember, there is a loan to repay...

Determine how and where you will obtain your best business

✓ How will the business be advertised?
- Will you make signs and post them? If so, be certain to comply with your township's rules for posting signs.
- Will you direct potential customers to an address or simply set up by the side of the road or at the end of your driveway?

✓ What is the estimated volume of drive-by and foot traffic for the possible locations of your stand? Perhaps you will hire a sibling to bark at passersby to increase business, announcing the unsurpassed deliciousness of your product – if so, remember to calculate their employment costs into your cost per serving...

Determine how you will grow your business

As Warren pointed out in his cost breakdown, he has plans to grow his business, so he may want to address within his business plan all that will go into furthering its growth. This may include:

Running the Corporation

- ✓ Exploring new ways of advertising, perhaps in partnership with the animal shelter with which he has chosen to share his profits
- ✓ Determining the percentage of profits which will be redirected towards growth costs
- ✓ Seeking ways to set his stand apart from any competition

Based upon the extent and quality of the business plan outline, the Director determines the level of funding to be provided (partial is recommended as it requires the wage earner to have their skin-in-the-game), and sets the terms for repayment. Those terms should include:

- ✓ **The time period of the loan.** The new business venture <u>must</u> have a timeline for repayment and that should be based upon the projected revenue. *Someday* is a not a reasonable repayment timeframe.
- ✓ **The interest rate of the loan.** When determining whether or not to charge interest, consideration should be given to the length of time of the loan (a shorter loan may not warrant any interest, for instance), the demonstrated reliability of the individual requesting

the loan (i.e., creditworthiness), and the amount of the loan (charging interest on a $20 loan may be more trouble than it is worth).

- ✓ **How the loan will be collateralized.** If the borrower has no funds in the bank with which to collateralize the loan, some alternate form of collateral should be determined.
- ✓ **Penalties for missed or late payments.** Missed or late payments must not go unnoticed. This will help provide a greater understanding by the borrower of the rules surrounding the extension of credit.
- ✓ **Circumstances under which the terms of the loan may be renegotiated.** If, for instance, Warren takes his loan in April, sets up his stand in May, and it proceeds to rain for the first four weeks of his venture, he may qualify for forgiveness of penalties associated with missed payments and be afforded the opportunity to renegotiate the terms of his loan. Proactively doing so will show his understanding of his responsibilities.

Warren's adherence to the terms of the loan will either be a direct reflection on his commitment to his business or point to the possibility of future issues with irresponsible credit behavior. Follow-through on the business and meeting the terms of the loan will establish the discipline needed to not only start meaningful (and sometimes risky) projects, but to see them through until they are complete.

If Warren had instead sought to fund the startup of a landscaping business, his initial funding capital requirement, and therefore the amount of his loan, would likely have been considerably higher. If he uses the loan to purchase a lawnmower and an initial tank of gas, as well as to rent the Household Corporation weed whacker, and then fails to earn any money from the venture, then forfeiture and sale of purchased items will need to be made to repay a part of the loan, he may be forced to interview for any open Household Corporation jobs, and his future earnings may be garnished in order to recoup the loss. Risks to the business and worst-case-scenario consequences should be taken into consideration when crafting the business plan.

Regardless of the scope of the business venture your wage earner is considering, the steps outlined in this section will prove helpful in the crucial business planning process. It is important to note, however, that developing a business plan is not the only outside activity a wage earner may find appealing. Their motivation may not be tied to financial gain and as such, you may wish to consider encouraging an *extracurricular career* path as an alternative. While fostering an extracurricular career path might seem like an odd concept, consider that developing a set of extracurricular interests may contribute to a new or wider social circle, a healthy lifestyle, an ability to effectively manage time and responsibilities, a sense of satisfaction in giving back, or even to simply becoming a well-rounded, interesting person. Extracurricular career paths might center on academics, athletics, charitable efforts, creative endeavors, entrepreneurial pursuits, personal health, to name a few.

In reality, most high school students who apply to colleges are *academically* qualified to attend the schools to which they apply – this is especially the case for prestigious Ivy League colleges. What sets a student apart from everyone else is what makes them *interesting*, and looking into what those kids do outside of their studies – whether that is starting a business, working a job, or pursuing an extracurricular activity – is as much a part of the college acceptance process as the ability to maintain a certain grade point average.

Regardless of whether your wage earner plans to go to college or elects instead to pursue entrepreneurship straight out of high school, encouraging them to follow what matters most to them is essential. This will reinforce your belief in their ability to think and plan for themselves, and foster in them a strong sense of self-worth.

> *"Do not train a child to learn by force or harshness; but direct them to it by what amuses their minds, so that you may be better able to discover with accuracy the peculiar bent of the genius of each."*
>
> – Plato, Philosopher

Bonus Opportunities

Bonuses should be financial in nature, and based upon what your Household Corporation can support from an overall financial perspective. The bonus structure will hinge upon your wage earner not only staying on track but going *above and beyond* what is expected of them.

There is an important implied meaning in that sentence, and at the risk becoming redundant, we have carved it into wood and screwed it into the book to outline that meaning here:

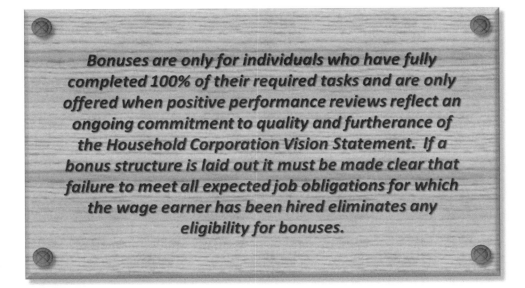

Bonuses are only for individuals who have fully completed 100% of their required tasks and are only offered when positive performance reviews reflect an ongoing commitment to quality and furtherance of the Household Corporation Vision Statement. If a bonus structure is laid out it must be made clear that failure to meet all expected job obligations for which the wage earner has been hired eliminates any eligibility for bonuses.

For those who feel the amount of attention drawn to that specific rule is over the top, it is done so in order to stress that going above and beyond what is expected is the **only** way to receive a bonus. If, for instance, the Meal Planning Assistant is doing a great job of devising menus, putting together shopping lists, and seeing to it that everything is on hand for the Household Cook, but has failed to make her bed on a daily basis or put her laundry away in a timely manner, she is not eligible for a bonus. It is essential that everyone be held to meeting the baseline duties of participating in the Household Corporation in addition to completing their specific job duties.

Unlike the incentives we discussed earlier to keep morale high, bonuses should be awarded on an individual basis and customized to the interests and motivating factors unique to that person. Following is a list of possible bonus opportunities that apply across a wide range of ages and interests.

Academic Focus

- ✓ Grades. *The Household Corporation Pays for As* – or bonuses may be based on cumulative GPA versus individual grades

- ✓ Reading. Reading self-assigned books at or above their grade level in school
- ✓ Vocabulary. Offer a small bonus (i.e., a quarter) for each four-syllable word used correctly in a sentence or for learning a new word per day

Athletic Focus

- ✓ Practice Regimen. Consistent practice regardless of weather, illness or even simply the desire to take a day off is certainly worth a reward
- ✓ Personal Achievement. Bonus on performance improvement such as increased shooting accuracy, pass completions or matches won; alternatively, merit awards and other forms of recognition may offer additional opportunities
- ✓ Good Sportsmanship. Younger kids might benefit from rewards tied to offering sincere congratulations to the winner at the end of a tough loss, staying out of fights, or remaining positive even while riding the bench

Charitable Focus

✓ Community Involvement. Initiating clean-up efforts and stirring members of the neighborhood/community to action is one example of a bonus opportunity

✓ Volunteer Work. Bonuses can be based on the number of hours spent volunteering, the number of organizations for which volunteer work is being performed, or even recognition for notable work

✓ Financial Donations. While it may seem counterintuitive to bonus on making charitable financial donations, bonuses may be provided as a 1:1 (or some other percentage) match of funds donated

Creative Focus

✓ Instrument Practice. As with athletic pursuits, practicing playing the violin, drums, saxophone, etc., can be rewarded for time spent or consistency in practicing

- ✓ Original Work. Producing short films, generating a body of artwork, writing original songs or poetry, or even authoring a book present opportunities for notable recognition
- ✓ Performances and Rehearsals. Whether cast in the lead role or as a member of the chorus, commitment to rehearsals and always giving top effort up to and through the performance shows dedication and should be rewarded

Entrepreneurial Focus

- ✓ Inventions. Whether creating a new computer program or the next modern convenience device, completion of the process of taking something from an initial idea to a prototype should be recognized as an achievement worthy of a bonus
- ✓ Business Ventures. In much the same way, launching a business venture – regardless of its ultimate success or failure, shows guts and follow-through, qualities which should be nurtured through bonuses
- ✓ Financial Management. Making wise decisions with money, paying off Household startup loans on time, saving and even investing may all deserve a reward

Ready to Launch

Health Focus

- ✓ Meal Planning. Consistent design of a healthy weekly meal plan for self or for family may be recognized when not a component of the individual's job description
- ✓ Exercise. Bonuses can be built on getting regular exercise when not participating in an organized sport (i.e., training for and running a 5K)
- ✓ Healthy Lifestyle Choices. Options for bonus opportunities, particularly for younger kids, can include time spent being active with friends versus watching television or playing video games or choosing healthy snacks over junk food; avoidance of fast food by teenagers may also be rewarded

These areas of focus are not mutually exclusive. They can be combined to help foster the growth of very well-rounded individuals with a wide variety of interests and pursuits. Bonuses can be in any amount – starting with just a nickel and working up to several dollars (or more, depending upon the funds available from Household income and the desire to reward at a higher dollar level). Bonuses should not, however, exceed the weekly wage, and should only be offered to those individuals who are fully employed by the Household Corporation and are receiving positive performance reviews. The frequency and parameters of bonus opportunities and bonuses must be consistent for all members of the Household and should be outlined, in detail, in the offer letter provided at the outset of employment.

Section 4

Fiscal Responsibility
Earning, Spending, Saving and Credit...

"Beware of little expenses; a small leak will sink a great ship."

– Benjamin Franklin, Founding Father and Inventor

Fiscal Responsibility – Earning, Spending, Saving and Credit…

Up until this point, we have discussed the business behind what goes into earning a dollar, how to build additional business opportunities and how to capitalize on bonus opportunities. Looking for a job, writing a resume, interviewing and ultimately getting hired into a position are all skills that will be utilized throughout your young wage earner's lifetime. While we touched on the idea of an incentivized savings and matching program in the job offer letter, we elected to wait until this key section to get into the nitty gritty behind passing along the idea of the value of a dollar earned.

In this day and age, with everything being electronic, very few kids ever have cause to actually handle paper money. Given the very nature of video and freemium phone-based games, money has become little more than a scorekeeping method which can be replaced by watching an advertisement or as in the example of one particular game, by shaking a tree (which only serves to teach the theory that money does, in fact, grow on trees). The wage your earner receives will ultimately come to represent the amount and quality of work they perform for the Household Corporation. In order to begin to restore the meaning and value of money, we strongly suggest that you pay them in *actual* cash. They should become familiar with currency – with the weight of a coin and the feel of a dollar bill. Payday should be a big deal, perhaps with each kid being handed an envelope containing their wages.

While kids should be permitted to ultimately make their own decisions with respect to their personal cash flow, a simple meeting, either with upper management or even a trusted financial friend or advisor prior to the receipt of their first weeks' pay, should be held to outline Household Corporation policy with respect to expectations for managing cash flow. How you elect to proceed from here will largely depend upon your own household resources and desire to teach (and perhaps learn) about saving and planning for the future; however, the basic tenets are the same regardless of the total household income and so we propose the following ideas.

Cash Flow, Budgeting and Goal-Setting

> *"A budget is telling your money where to go rather than wondering where it went."*
> – John C. Maxwell, Author and Speaker

We are assuming that your kids' basic needs (i.e., clothing, food, shelter, etc.) are being met and supplied by the Household Corporation, and as such, they will have no need to save up for, say, underwear.

Consider this hypothetical situation: Suppose your kid is in the mall where she sees a pair of knee-socks emblazoned with pandas, which would make an amazing addition to her sweet panda-themed collection, but are otherwise not *needed*... She looks at the price of the socks and learns they are $14.95, which with tax will total approximately $16.00.

She turns her angel face up to you, and says "can I get them, pleeeeeeease???"

You have a few options:

1. You can get them for her and be The Best Parent Ever, at least until you leave the mall and mistakenly turn on top 40 radio in the car which results in a pronounced eye roll and a silent ride home. She has learned little in this situation, aside from the fact that she can probably work you over again in the future.

2. You can ask her how much cash she has in her wallet. In one case, she may say she has failed to bring her wallet along – to which you could reply in a mock-shocked tone (preferably with some affectation of a teenaged girl's voice), "I can't believe you, *like,* came to the mall without your money!?!?!?" and resume walking past the store. In this situation, she has learned to bring her own money to the mall.

3. In the case where she has indeed brought her wallet, she checks to see what she has, and it turns out she has $8.00. She makes a bi-weekly wage of $4.00 as your Laundry Manager and as she has come to understand what goes into earning those dollars, she says, "I've got $8.00 – it's going to be a month before I'll have enough to buy them, I guess we can just go." If this is indeed her response, you have already gotten through to her and begun the process of teaching her to be fiscally considerate. You understand that in retail, fashions (and what is in stock) can come and go quite

quickly. What is available today might not be available tomorrow, so here, you have a couple additional options:

a. *Layaway.* Under the layaway scenario, you purchase the socks with $8.00 from her and another $8.00 of your own; you keep the socks in the bag, with the receipt and the tags still attached, and upon your receipt of the remaining $8.00, she is given the fully paid for socks.

b. *I'm In For Half.* Under this option, you can elect to incentivize your child to always pitch in half of the cost of anything extraneous that will still serve a purpose (stuffed animals and video games should probably not fall under this rule; however, how and whether you elect to implement this is entirely your call). Keep in mind thought that this should be laid out to your wage earners, and offered equally to all of them, at the outset of the Corporation, rather than when someone sees something they want.

c. *Log some overtime.* In this case, some prep work will have been necessary. On the Job Postings board, there should always be a list of opportunities for extra work – projects that do not represent daily, weekly or even monthly responsibilities, but that may require a large amount of work for a very short period of time (i.e., cleaning out the garage). These projects should already have an overtime wage associated with them in order to avoid the random assignment of value (say, $8.00, for instance) to the project. If she wants to exercise this option, she may need to call management to determine whether opportunities are available and if so, the going rate for those jobs, in order to make the most informed decision.

In any of the options above, your kid should still be asked to consider whether she wants the socks badly enough to spend two months' wages on them (or one, in the *I'm In For Half* scenario). If she makes the decision to do so, remember that follow-through is key on your part if she chooses the layaway option. Also, an important note here: you should not question her final decision, as that will only serve to teach her that you have doubts about her decision-making process, which may lead to difficulty in her making similar decisions in the future. She should be encouraged to develop confidence in making choices with respect to her own finances.

Not every spending decision made by your young wage earners will require such thought. They may choose to buy a snack while at the public pool or a pack of gum from the grocery store. Managing their personal cash flow and making decisions with respect to their own money should become a part of their day-to-day lives. While it may prove tempting to point out, each time your wage earner purchases something, that the money in their wallet is all they have and if they spend it this week they will have nothing left next week, this should be avoided at all costs. If this occurs, and next week, they have run themselves out of money, they should experience that for themselves. And yes, this may mean they are the only one of your kids to not get a snack at the pool – but that is what the real world will eventually feel like and better to learn the lesson now with a snack-sized bag of pretzels at the pool versus the rent money.

What often happens in this situation is that someone – a parent, a grandparent, the chaperone or even a sibling – may offer to buy the broke kid a bag of pretzels because they feel bad for them. The person buying the extra pretzels sees the gesture as one of kindness, perhaps extended to relieve themselves of the guilt of seeing someone go without. Just like with dad in the car, the kid without the money has just learned that they can guilt someone into giving them something and they themselves do not need to be responsible with their own money. In writing this section, we discussed whether this would discourage being charitable, which brings up the necessity to define the difference between charity and enabling. ***Charity is providing something to someone otherwise unable to earn it, whereas enabling is doing the same for someone who simply does not want to work for it, which is behavior that should be discouraged at all costs.***

Rather than buying a bag of pretzels, this is an opportunity to teach another lesson on the extension of credit. If a kid is going to loan his sibling $1.25 for a bag of pretzels at the pool, he should consider the creditworthiness of his sibling. Does the sibling also hold a job with the Household Corporation? What is his job performance like – does he get all his work done or is it possible he did not get paid due to poor performance? Is the sibling just down on his luck or is he seemingly always out of money? All of these facts and factors should be considered by the individual looking to ensure that everyone has a bag of pretzels. If

Fiscal Responsibility – Earning, Spending, Saving and Credit…

it is determined that the kid in question is just down on his luck, had a big unexpected expense last week (had to replace the trucks on his competition skateboard), and is good for the loan, then the extension of credit is a good idea, but should be extended in writing with terms for repayment. Those terms can be very simple:

I, Warren, am loaning Jimmy $1.25 today, April 1, 2016, for a bag of pretzels. Jimmy agrees to pay me back, in full, on April 15th (our next payday). If he doesn't pay on time, he owes me $1.50.

Both Warren and Jimmy should sign the note and file it with the Financial Officer of the Household Corporation, if they feel it is necessary. If Jimmy is a good kid, he will pay Warren back on the 15th. If he is sneaky, he might try to "forget" the note and just wait to see if Warren mentions it. If Jimmy fails to make good on his repayment, the head of the Household should be made aware and Jimmy's paycheck should be docked in the following pay period.

With thoughtful spending and conscientious, responsible lending comes the idea of budgeting. To be clear, budgeting is not the same as understanding your cash flow – these two are often confused and something we, as financial professionals, see on a daily basis with very savvy individuals. Cash flow simply represents that (and certainly where) your money is being spent. Understanding this can be as simple as keeping all receipts and then sorting them into piles for groceries, dining out, clothing, gas for the car and so on. This is helpful when determining what your financial priorities have been *historically*. Developing and working within a budget instead considers your financial priorities *going forward.* Budgeting is goal oriented, versus the simple data-gathering nature of determining cash flow.

Take the case of Jimmy who had to borrow $1.25 from Warren for a bag of pretzels at the pool. This is not the first time that the family has gone to the pool, and in fact, it is common practice for them to do so, as they have every Saturday, all summer long. As this is a regularly scheduled occurrence, and Jimmy routinely likes to have a bag of pretzels while at the pool, he should have *budgeted* the $1.25 to purchase them. If Jimmy only understands his cash flow, he simply knows that he spent the money somewhere else. Jimmy may be a spendthrift – irresponsible and extravagant with little concern for where he gets his pretzel money, or he may be decidedly frugal and merely a victim of circumstance – the circumstance that led to his cracked skateboard trucks and the subsequent purchase of a replacement set. Either way, Jimmy would benefit from a lesson in budgeting, which again, involves setting financial priorities and making a plan to stick to them.

The first step in creating a budget is knowing how much and when you get paid.

The next step, whether you have one fixed expense (a $1.25 bag of pretzels every Saturday) or a whole household and lifestyle of them (rent, insurance, utilities, taxes, etc.) is to determine what has to be paid and with what frequency. This does not have to be fancy. There is no need to run out and purchase accounting or bookkeeping software or even a computer to get this process going. If you have a piece of paper and a pencil and possibly a calculator, in the event subtraction trips you up on

Fiscal Responsibility – Earning, Spending, Saving and Credit...

occasion, you have all the tools necessary to proceed. So for Jimmy, his paper will look like this:

My budget stuff		
What I make	$10	Every other week
What I spend		
Pretzel money at the pool	$1.25	Every week

In order to determine what Jimmy has left over to spend, he next will need to make sure that all the numbers represent the same time period. Since the pay period is when his money comes in, we suggest making that the consistent time period, which means Jimmy's paper will be adjusted to look like this:

My budget stuff		
What I make	$10	Every other week
What I spend		
Pretzel money at the pool*	$2.50	Every other week
*I spend $1.25 each week on pretzels		

Since pretzel money is Jimmy's only fixed expense, his resulting free cash flow is $7.50 every other week.

My budget stuff		
What I make	$10	Every other week
What I spend		
Pretzel money at the pool*	$2.50	Every other week
*I spend $1.25 each week on pretzels		
What I have left over every two weeks	$7.50	

Ready to Launch

For the sake of this example, we are going to assume that Jimmy has learned the valued lessons of earning and saving money and that he has simply fallen on difficult circumstances, causing him to utilize his saved dollars to buy new trucks for his skateboard. While prior to going through the exercise above, Jimmy had simply set aside his unspent dollars (whatever they wound up being for any given two-week period) in an envelope in his sock drawer, he was unaware of his actual cash flow. He now knows that he has an extra $7.50 every two weeks and can determine what he would like to do with those dollars, either in the short-term or over a longer period of time. Some quick math tells him that $7.50 every other week adds up to $195 over the course of a year and that suddenly sounds like a lot of money to him.

While Jimmy did run short by $1.25 for the week and resorted to taking a loan from his brother, he clearly had some money set aside to buy new trucks for his skateboard – an extravagance that runs around $20 apiece for the brand he prefers. Jimmy had saved at least $30 prior to this week's salary in order to afford the $40 expenditure. Going forward, in order to begin his sock drawer savings anew, he will first need to account for both the current and next weeks' pretzel budget, as well as a full repayment of the loan he took from Warren.

As time passes, Jimmy's fixed expenses will likely change and with it, so will the availability of uncommitted dollars. If Jimmy has this system in place as those expenses and his income change over time, he will be able to use the simple basics of budgeting to ensure his fixed expenses are covered and he is aware of his free cash flow and get to the real business of planning for his future.

Fiscal Responsibility – Earning, Spending, Saving and Credit...

With planning for the future in mind, we can move on to goal-setting. By determining longer-term goals (beyond next week's pretzels), how and where dollars are saved becomes nearly as important as the simple fact *that* they are being saved.

Whether this is done as a meeting with management, during a periodic performance review, or independently, each kid should be encouraged to come up with a set of goals. Those goals may be personal, academic, professional (like Warren's goal to grow his lemonade stand business), or simply financial in nature (like saving to a targeted number of dollars), or certainly a combination of all of these and more. A simple goal-setting worksheet should include a timeframe for each goal, as well as any associated costs or prerequisites, and may look something like this :

My goals

Stuff I want to buy	How much	When
New Tony Hawk skateboard	$90	6-8 months
New longboard (don't know which yet)	$120	12-18 months
A car (used is fine for my first)	$3000	6-7 years
Stuff I want to do		
Go indoor skydiving	$70	12-18 months
See Bruno Mars (my hero) in concert	$170	12-18 months
Go real skydiving (if mom lets me)	$300	6-7 years
Go to the X games (wherever it is!)	No idea!	Someday

Jimmy has clearly put a lot of thought into his goals, and nearly all of them have an associated cost and timeframe for attaining them. His timeframe for several goals overlap one another, so in calculating his projected budget allocations, he will need to consider them all

Ready to Launch

simultaneously. Due to the fact that some of his goals have a longer time horizon (when he ultimately needs the money), he can prioritize the more immediate goals first, and then reallocate those previously saved dollars as the goals are met and paid for.

He has set four goals within six to eighteen months, with the Tony Hawk skateboard in the near term of 6-8 months. We will lay this out, starting with the skateboard. While there are technically 26 pay periods in a year when the Household Corporation pays wage earners every other week, for the sake of laying this out, we will use the more conservative two pay periods per month on which to base projections. We are also assuming that Jimmy's Household Corporation does not offer the *I'm In For Half* program which would only require him to save up half the cost.

In order to save up for the skateboard in 6 months, that equates to 12 pay periods into which the $90 must be divided, versus 16 pay periods for an 8-month target date of purchase. If Jimmy wants the board in 6 months, he will need to save $7.50 per pay period. As shown earlier, he does presently have a surplus of $7.50 per pay period when his weekly pretzel expense is figured in; however, this does not take into account the repayment of his loan to Warren or any other unplanned expenses that may arise in the meantime. As such, it is likely a better idea for Jimmy to extend out his savings over the 16 pay periods in 8 months, which equates to $5.63 saved per pay period towards this goal. If he elects to go this route, he will be left with $1.87 per pay period that he can allocate to other goals or to current cash flow needs.

Jimmy's next three goals all share a common timeframe – one of 12-18 months. Using the method laid out above (and the leftover cash), Jimmy has $29.92 saved towards all three of these goals collectively at the end of the first 8 months of the 12-18 month timeframe, provided he does not spend his surplus cash. This leaves him with 4-10 months – or 8-20 pay periods – to save for these longer-term goals. The total amount he is going to need to cover all three of them is $360. If he successfully saves the $29.92 from the first 8 months of his saving strategy and applies this to the $360, that leaves him with $330.08 to earn in 4-10 months.

To save for each of the three 12-18 month goals simultaneously with a target of 12 months (rather than 18) requires saving $41.26 per pay period, and Jimmy only earns $10.00. To do so at the 18-month mark requires saving $16.51 per pay period. Again, it seems that Jimmy falls short. He can consider several options at this point:

1. He can save for one goal at a time and fulfill them as they are funded
2. He can adjust his timeframe for one or more of his goals
3. He can cut out pretzels at the pool
4. He can seek out other opportunities to earn money – perhaps picking up an Odd Job from the Job posting board, developing an outside business activity, or even working for Warren at the now flourishing lemonade stand

This process can be repeated for each of Jimmy's goals, and in fact the goal of saving $3,000 towards the purchase of a new car, if done over 26 pay periods per year for seven years, amounts to a savings goal of $16.49 per month – which is virtually the same rate of savings as that which he will already be employing to meet his 12-18 month goals! Of course, for those first ten months where his goal funding overlaps, he will need to save $33 per pay period. It should be noted that Jimmy will be unable to fund his goal of attending the X Games, given that he has neither assigned a dollar amount to the goal, nor has he set a timeframe for allocating savings towards it – as noted previously *someday* is not a measurable amount of time, and does not afford the goal-setter the opportunity to develop a plan.

Or, he can turn to saving somewhere other than his sock drawer envelope…

Saving, Matching and Vesting

We hinted at incentivized savings in the Benefits portion of the Job Offer letter. What that ultimately looks like in your own Household Corporation hinges on the discretionary dollars available to the Corporation at large. If you feel that you would like to create an incentivized savings plan, but do not feel you have the resources to do so, consider that you might reduce the salaries paid for any given job in order to further sweeten the deal for your savers. Without explanation, we are fairly certain this will seem vague.

While not every kid will have a clear-cut set of financial goals like Jimmy, that does not mean they should not be incentivized to save their hard-earned dollars. This will not only teach them to not spend their money like drunken sailors on shore leave, but will also serve to show them the value of compounding and while also imparting the underlying idea of qualified employer contribution plans.

Before you get started with a savings plan for any of your young wage earners, you will need to go through the process of opening an account for them. Banks offer a number of different ownership structures for setting up accounts for kids, with options for joint ownership, individual ownership by the kid, ownership by the kid that allows them access at age 18 (or the age of majority in your home state), or gifting accounts. We strongly suggest you consult with your CPA or tax professional, your banker, or a financial advisor with strong integrity when making this decision, as there are various consequences that can arise from setting up accounts in certain ways, which include some of the following:

- ✓ Inclusion in asset review when being considered for federal financial aid to attend college
- ✓ Party to whom the tax burden passes on any interest earned
- ✓ Who is able to make withdrawals from the account
- ✓ Who makes decisions with respect to how or whether the money is invested

While your team of financial professionals may feel differently about this, we strongly suggest that the account not be held jointly. All too often, we have seen where well-intending parents, grandparents and other custodians have dipped into the kid's account to meet a short-term financial need and then have failed to return the "borrowed" funds. If you are in need of borrowing from the wage earner's account, you may want to review your own cash flow and budgeting, as changes may need to be made. Teaching is best done by setting a good example.

So in the spirit of good examples, following is a visual outline of what matched savings might look like once you have set up your wage earner's account. After that, we will explain.

Fiscal Responsibility – Earning, Spending, Saving and Credit...

Name	Periodic Wage	Earner Savings	Household Match (10%)	Total Deposit	Match Forfeiture	Vesting Period
Jimmy	$10.00	$7.50	$0.75	$8.25	6 months	7 years

In the example above, Jimmy receives a bi-weekly wage of $10. He is electing to deposit $7.50 of his wage into his savings account. Because the Household Corporation offers a 10% match of any contribution to savings, Jimmy receives an additional deposit of $0.75 (or 10% of his $7.50 deposit) from the Household Corporation. This essentially turns his $10 wage into one totaling $10.75. There is a catch, of course – just as with company savings plans, the Household Corporation plan carries with it a vesting schedule and match forfeiture.

While Jimmy is permitted to remove his portion of his account at any point following the deposit of his funds, there may be penalties for doing so, as this Household Corporation plan carries with it a six-month match forfeiture in addition to a 7 year vesting schedule for Jimmy. As Jimmy is now eleven years old, he will be fully vested (or able to take control of 100% of the value of his account) once he reaches 18. The six-month match forfeiture is in place to close the potential loophole of depositing money into the savings account solely for the purpose of obtaining the matched dollars and then withdrawing all or a portion of the savings on which the match is based. We feel that six months is likely sufficient; however, as with the wages, the match percentage (or the existence of a match at all) and the vesting schedule, these are all left to your discretion.

If the plan above represents Jimmy's Household matching plan, we should return to Jimmy's goals. He has a 6-8 month goal of affording and purchasing the Tony Hawk skateboard. If he elects to participate in the incentivized savings program while reaching his goal, he will need to keep in mind that the soonest he will be able to withdraw his money and retain the 10% match is at six months, but by doing so, he will have managed to save an additional $9 in those same six months, to which he will have access at 18. If he does this for a full seven years, with consistent savings of $7.50 per month, the Household Corporation will provide him with an additional $136.50 in "unearned" dollars.

In this example, the vesting schedule is tied to Jimmy reaching age 18, which we have elected to use for the simplicity of it. You may wish to tie your Household Corporation vesting schedule to different milestones (or even more than one), or if you want to be even more creative, you may allow for a percentage of vesting for each A or B attained on the kid's report card. Regardless of how you ultimately set up the vesting schedule, incentivized savings will require some basic bookkeeping skills in order to prevent losing track of the kid's contribution and the Household match, as well as the vesting timeline. This will need to be completed for each wage earner separately. A Savings Match and Vesting Worksheet is included in the Appendix on which to base your own.

Investing

"Compound interest is the eighth wonder of the world. He who understands it, earns it; he who doesn't, pays it."
— Albert Einstein, Physicist and Mathematician

Now that your wage earner has been incentivized to save a portion of his hard-earned salary, it may be time to touch upon investing. Investing can be a way to further enhance the value of a dollar saved; however, it should also be noted before we go any further, that **all** investing carries with it the risk of loss. While many investment advisers may say that the risk of loss over time is minimal, given the long-term investment timeframe for your young wage earner, we feel that taking on undue risks in investments – even at a young age when there may be considerable time to potentially recoup any losses – is not always wise, or even necessary. There are no investment recommendations to be found here, but rather a list of considerations with respect to understanding investing, risk and due diligence when it comes to seeking out help in this regard.

Many investors put off saving for retirement until they are established in a career, have purchased a home or a car, and still more until after they have started a family. It is assumed that because there are so many years between high school graduation and retirement that there is sufficient time to make up the difference later. Let's go back to Jimmy. At 18, after high school graduation, his goals have changed somewhat, and look much farther down the road:

Ready to Launch

	My goals	
Stuff I want to buy	How much	When
New car	$27,000	4 years
Condo	$140,000	7 years
A house	$235,000	12 years
Stuff I want to do		
Go to Europe	$4,000	5 years
Get married (nice wedding)	$5,000	8-10 years
Retire (at 68 at the latest)	$1,500,000	50 years
Meet Bruno Mars (still my hero)	PRICELESS	Someday

While previously, Jimmy's list had the goal to purchase a used car for around $3,000, his list of long-term goals, now that he is 18, has a much higher price tag. Saving for retirement alone runs him $2,500 per month for the next fifty years, in order to achieve his goal of $1.5MM in savings. This assumes that Jimmy is saving in a traditional bank savings account, which at present, earns only nominal interest. If Jimmy elects to invest those dollars, at a conservative rate of return of 3.00%, over the same 50 years, he only needs to save $1,100 per month to reach the same goal. Of course, the 3.00% is not a guarantee and is exposed to market risk, unlike those dollars at the bank.

Investing is more complex than simply putting money into an investment account; however, and should be undertaken with prudence. First-time investors – whether that is you or your young wage earner – should begin with an understanding of a few terms, which we have taken the time to explain in plain English below:

✓ **Risk Tolerance**. While risk is not always fully calculable, what you or your wage earner are willing to accept, is. By way of example, consider that the speedometer in most vehicles tops out around 160 miles per hour. Most people are not inclined to drive that fast, given the associated risks of doing so, which can include getting a speeding ticket at the felony level, the possibility of hitting another vehicle if done in traffic, the possibility of loss of control of the vehicle at that speed, or the likelihood of severe injury or death were an accident to occur at that speed. Knowing that you do not care to drive above the posted speed limit, or that you prefer to drive even slower at times, represents an understanding of your personal risk attitude with respect to driving. The same kind of risk consideration should come into play when investing, which means not just hearing, but fully *understanding* the risks associated with investing. Considering how much of your hard-earned, hard-saved money you may lose at a moment's notice and may never have the opportunity to recover, is a good start – because risk is about loss. For instance, when weighing whether to drive 160 miles per hour, thinking of how many minutes you will conserve on the way to the PTA meeting is not likely where the logic process begins.

✓ **Results Not Typical**. In the example above, consider that while most people do not look to drive 160 miles per hour, some certainly do. Those with the means and the risk attitude to do so may even elect to pursue a career in auto racing, ultimately driving at speeds in excess of 200 miles per hour. Some of those will go on to careers as drivers in the Indianapolis 500, and each year, one person will win. Basing the decision to drive 160 miles per hour on the success of that single winner fails to take into consideration the results of the 32 other drivers who failed to win, as well as the number who may have crashed or even died during the race. It is important to ensure that you are reviewing all available data when making investment decisions, rather than studying cherry-picked results geared towards making risk-taking appear attractive or less risky than in actuality. Always ask for a representation of typical results.

- ✓ **Time Horizon.** This is how long you have to let your investment grow and ties back into your goals. Having a long time horizon however does not necessarily equate to having the ability or desire to take on greater risk. It is often suggested that with a long time horizon (say, 45 years until retirement), the investor has sufficient time to make up for any substantially poor-performing years and recoup any losses incurred during those market cycles. While that may indeed be the case, something else to keep in mind is the fact that a poor-performing year may create a significant enough setback that taking on ever-increasing amounts of risk may become attractive in an attempt to arrive at the original outcome within the original timeframe.

Imagine the Smiths and Jones families elect to take a road trip from Hoboken, New Jersey to the Indianapolis 500 in Indianapolis, Indiana. Depending upon which route the each family takes, the drive time is projected to be between 10 hours and 33 minutes and 11 hours and 23 minutes. The race will be kicking off at noon on Sunday, and everyone wants to be there for

Fiscal Responsibility – Earning, Spending, Saving and Credit…

the big parade beforehand. Both Mr. Smith and Mr. Jones have available vacation days and their kids are all doing well enough in school that they can miss the Friday prior to the race.

Mr. Smith takes a vacation day and he and his two boys sleep in on Friday morning, have a home-cooked breakfast, pack a lunch and hit the road at 10:00 a.m. They pop in the John Denver anthology they have collectively compiled and run into construction just outside of Newark. Despite the 30-minute delay, they are still enjoying themselves. They continue on, leaving their home state and making it halfway across Pennsylvania, when just outside of Harrisburg, the Check Engine light comes on. Mr. Smith pulls off the highway, stops at a gas station to inquire about the nearest mechanic and by 2:30, the car is being looked at. The mechanic changes the oil and the light is resolved and they are back on the road.

Since they were originally on track to arrive at Aunt Cheryl's in Wheeling, Ohio at 5:30 p.m. for dinner, Mr. Smith gives her a call and tells her of the delay. They wind up arriving at 7:30 p.m. and Cheryl reheats the leftovers. They enjoy a nice evening, catching up, playing cards and then get to bed at a reasonable hour. They once again wake at their leisure and enjoy good food and company for breakfast, get a hot shower and hit the road, refreshed, at 10:00 a.m. They then arrive in Indianapolis just as their reserved hotel allows for check-in, where they unpack, get the lay of the land, and set out to find the best Indiana Hoosier Sugar Cream Pie they can find. They enjoy their evening, get back to the hotel with full bellies and high excitement for the following day, and get a good night's sleep. They are up at 7:00 a.m. and off to participate in all the pre-race activities.

Meanwhile...

Mr. Jones has decided he will save his vacation day for use in the summer and elects to leave at noon on Saturday. Warren and Jimmy argue that they should leave earlier, since that will have them arriving in Indianapolis after 10:30 p.m., and they are concerned about being too tired to get up for the parade. Mr. Jones says they are welcome to sleep in the car and that should keep them from being too tired. At noon on Saturday, the car is fully loaded and with a great deal of excitement, the three pile in to the car. They pop in the Pearl Jam anthology they have collectively compiled and run into construction just outside of Newark. After a 30-minute delay, Mr. Jones says, "nothing to worry about – we'll make up the time now since we're on the highway," and begins speeding in an attempt to gain ground more quickly. Just outside of Allentown, he is pulled over. The boys spend twenty minutes on the side of the road, erasing all the time Mr. Jones felt he had made up by speeding, still leaving them behind by a half hour, and costing him an unexpected $52.50.

Mr. Jones pulls back into traffic with Warren and Jimmy reminding him not to speed. They all agree they are back on track with only a small loss of time, and hours of Eddie Vedder remaining in queue. An hour and half later, just outside of Harrisburg, the Check Engine light comes on. They pull off the highway, stop at a gas station to inquire about the nearest mechanic and learn that there are few options available at 3:30 p.m. on a Saturday. A gas station attendant provides them with the nearest open mechanic, and by 4:00, they are in line for service. After an hour wait, the car is finally taken in for service and following a seemingly endless additional half hour of waiting, the mechanic returns and tells Mr. Jones that after hooking the car up to their diagnostic computer, they were unable to find anything but that the car should probably have an oil change.

As they leave the mechanic, it is 6:00 p.m. and the boys are starving, so they ask if they can stop for food. Mr. Jones agrees that they can stop, but adds that it will only be for snacks because now, even without stopping, they will arrive at their hotel after 2:00 a.m. While at the checkout counter at the convenience store, the boys are making noise about all the lost time and expressing some disappointment about the fact that they did not set out the day before. Mr. Jones comments that they would still have encountered construction and the Check Engine light with the car. The boys agree but point out that neither of those would have been very troublesome if they had a whole extra day to travel, and then remind their dad he also lost them 20 minutes by speeding and getting a ticket. He argues that his speeding made up 20 minutes initially, so getting pulled over really did not lose them any time, to which Warren replies, "but it did cost you fifty bucks." The cashier overhears the conversation and suggests that if they stay off the highway and follow his personally-designed route, they will definitely not encounter the police and can easily cruise at well above the speed limit, making up hours in lost time, guaranteed.

While Jimmy sets to calculating just how quickly they would have to drive in order to make up for three lost hours, his dad pays the man, jots down the route and they head back to the car. As they turn out of the convenience store, clearly following the clerk's instructions, Jimmy attempts to bring the math to his dad's attention but is told to eat his beef jerky and enjoy the ride.

Mr. Jones gets onto the suggested route and kicks his speed up to 80 miles per hour, 25 higher than the posted limit, taking corners at speeds that have the boys in the back feeling very uncomfortable. After twenty miles of clear sailing, the Jones family crests a hill where Pennsylvania's finest once again pull him over for speeding. Twenty additional minutes are lost, along with a fine this time of $172. Warren and Jimmy are silent in the back seat, and Mr. Jones, both embarrassed and annoyed, gets back to driving – this time at the posted speed limit.

Nine silent hours later, at 3:32 a.m., they pull into the hotel. They unload their bags onto a bellhop cart and head to the counter to check in, where they learn that reservations are only held until midnight unless the guest calls to reconfirm their arrival. There room has been given to another patron and there are no available rooms. Mr. Jones asks if there are any other hotels the manager can recommend and is told that the whole town has been sold out for months because of the race. In disbelief, he calls around to several hotels and motels and by 4:00 a.m., he lets the boys know they are going to have to sleep in the car.

Fiscal Responsibility – Earning, Spending, Saving and Credit...

When they wake up, in the parking lot of the hotel, it is 1:30 p.m. on Sunday. They have missed the parade, the first ninety minutes of the race, have not had a meal since leaving Hoboken, have no way to shower, and have to walk eight blocks to the speedway. They are all silent as they enter the speedway and make their way to their seats. The Smiths, as it turns out, are sitting immediately next to them, rested, decked out in full souvenir gear, and going on about how eleven drivers went out in the first three laps of the race.

While both the Smiths and the Jones started out with the same time horizon, their decisions with respect to risk, results, and whose advice to follow directly affected the outcome of their trip. Both encountered the identical unforeseen events, but the Smiths capitalized on their opportunity for an early start, despite that meaning that Mr. Smith would have one less vacation day come Christmas, and were able to work around those events and still make it to the race with plenty of time to enjoy themselves. Mr. Jones, on the other hand, chose to save his day off and then made risky choices based on his need to make up for the time he had lost due to those same unforeseen events. As a result, not only did the Jones family sleep in the car, but they missed the race entirely.

The long and the short of it is this: having a longer time horizon may afford you the option of not engaging in undue risk-taking with respect to investing, provided you use that time wisely, have a plan in mind, and the discipline to stick to it.

"Save a part of your income and begin now, for the man with a surplus controls circumstances and the man without a surplus is controlled by circumstances."
— Henry Buckley, Australian Politician

✓ **Investment Objective.** This is simply what you want your money to do. While most people will say that they just want their money to grow, that is insufficient data on which to form an investment strategy. The investment objective should be framed within the time horizon and the risk tolerance of the investor, so an example of an investment objective is: *I would like my money to grow for ten years with very little exposure to market fluctuations.* Whomever is choosing your investments – be that yourself or a professional investment manager – should be able to provide you with the likelihood of reaching your goals, given all the facts under consideration. An objective is a *target*, not a *guarantee*, and forming an appropriate expectation with respect to whether or not the goal can be attained, may lead to thoughtful consideration of setting realistic financial goals and reasonable timeframes. Adjustments may need to be made in spending or saving or timeframe for any given goal in order to increase the likelihood of reaching financial goals within the investor's comfort level (i.e., risk tolerance), rather than simply taking on more risk and essentially rolling the dice on future outcomes, as outlined in the comparison between the Smiths' and Joneses' trips to Indianapolis.

Fiscal Responsibility – Earning, Spending, Saving and Credit...

- ✓ **Guarantee**. There are no free lunches, and there are no guarantees, especially not in the financial/investment industry. If you receive an invitation from an investment professional that includes a free meal, know that a sales pitch is absolutely, without question, included with or immediately following that meal. Likewise, if anyone purports a guaranteed return, know they are selling a very specific investment product, and costs of that guarantee (both in terms of dollars and time commitment of the investment) must be taken under extremely careful consideration by you or your young wage earner prior to moving forward. We strongly suggest that if you hear someone in the investment industry use this word, you get a second, unaffiliated professional opinion on what they are offering.

- ✓ **Commissions, Loads and Fees**. Regardless of how, where or with whom you elect to invest, understand that there are always costs associated with doing so. To clear up the confusion with respect to the terms noted, *commissions* are a percentage of proceeds earned by a person selling a product (think: what the realtor makes for selling you a house); *loads* are dollars earned by the managers of select investment products (think: what the management company of your apartment building makes as its cut of your rent); and, *fees* are charged by someone hired to provide investors with advice (think: what you would pay someone to tell you all the best places to live and then pick one for you based on how well they know you). Understanding what you are paying for is essential and should be outlined in detail by anyone with whom you invest. Consider requesting an itemized estimation of out-of-pocket costs to you, as well as any asset-based fees and expenses your accounts may incur that may otherwise go unnoticed. In addition, if that person does not have an in-depth, clear understanding of your personal, individual needs and goals, as well as your actual appetite for risk, they should not be paid to provide you with customized planning and advice, as no two situations are alike and investment selection should be based on your unique situation.

✓ **Equities, Fixed Income and Derivatives**. While the types and "packages" of investments are too extensive to outline here and to do so would risk constituting specific investment recommendations, it is important to understand a few simple terms, as the bulk of investments will fall into a few different categories. Those that tie into owning a piece of a company are called *equities*. Investing in *fixed income* means you own a piece of a loan or a debt owed, and can expect to receive some form of dividend for doing so. *Derivatives* are vastly more complicated, but are essentially derived or created from other types of investments and therefore should be explained in great detail by anyone marketing them to you. Any time you elect to invest, it is essential that you have a clear understanding of what you own. A good rule of thumb is that if your investment adviser cannot explain it in detail but such that you understand it, it may be wise to seek a second professional opinion.

✓ **Fiduciary Responsibility**. When an investment professional assumes fiduciary responsibility over some or all of your investable assets, they are *required by law* to act in your best interest. While this may seem like a no-brainer, not all decisions made within the investment industry reflect the best interest of the retail client. Confirm who is responsible for which fees (i.e., trade charges) and whether the decision to retain a position is tied to costs incurred by either you or your advisor. If they are assuming fiduciary responsibility, it should be outlined to you in writing.

✓ **Golden Unicorn.** This is our term for when something appears to be too good to be true. Whether you have received an email from a prince in Africa, a call from the department of antiquities as it relates to assets recovered from a world war, or an offer to buy shares in a company that no longer exists or a movie that was already made, be assured it is not real. A return on investment of 25%, for instance, is extremely uncommon, and sustaining that level of return over a prolonged period is nearly impossible. If it seems too good to be true, it is – even if your next door neighbor is telling you how much money they have made on it.

As reflected in the example of Jimmy's goal of reaching retirement with $1.5MM in savings and the differing methods in which he can save those dollars, a slow and steady approach to investing could save him upwards of $1,400 per month versus simply saving his dollars in the bank. Finding someone trustworthy with whom to invest those dollars; however, may prove a bit more difficult.

> *"Don't play games that you don't understand, even if you see lots of other people making money from them."*
> – Tony Hsieh, CEO of Zappos

Ready to Launch

As we discussed in the introduction, this book was written after spending a day with a group of eighth graders who had undertaken an investment project wherein they formed teams of investors (four students per team), selected a handful of investments (their choices were limited to the stock market), and then tracked the performance of their collective investment portfolios over a period of several months.

While their investment selections were limited to equities as noted, upon asking why they had selected the names they had for their portfolio, each team responded with one of the following statements: *"we buy their products," "we use their services," "we go to their stores"* or simply, *"we think they're cool."* Despite only being in the eighth grade, these kids inherently understand that buying something they believe in and use themselves is an excellent place to start the due diligence process when it comes to investing.

If building an investment portfolio for yourself or your kid feels outside your comfort zone, you may elect to find a trusted investment advisor with whom to work. If the Director of the Household *has a guy*, it stands to reason that advisor may be the first choice. On the other hand, if this is yours (or your kid's) first foray into investing, here are a few points of consideration that might be helpful while you interview possible advisors:

1. ***How does the advisor make their money?*** This goes back to the fees and commissions discussed earlier – a reputable advisor will be able to outline the exact costs incurred by you and your young investor as well as the income earned by him. If the fee is based upon the value of the account (i.e., 1.00 – 2.00% of the total

value), it might be prudent to ask for a flat fee option, given that as the account grows, so does the amount paid by you or your young investor, which may prove counterintuitive, particularly as new contributions are invested and the account grows. For instance, if the investment advice being offered on $5,000 is worth $50-100 per year; should a substantially similar portfolio (i.e., the same investments, but in higher amounts) valued at $50,000 cost $500-1,000, given that the advice being provided is essentially the same?

2. ***What do you get for what you are paying?*** Knowing how your advisor earns a living and knowing what you get for your hard-earned dollars are two completely different things. If the advisor holds himself out as a *Planner – whether certified or not –* then there should be an element of discovery and planning to the services for which you are paying. A Planner should plan *with* you, not *for* you. Failure on the part of any investment professional (regardless of whether they are simply picking investments or working in a full planning capacity) to get to know you and/or your young wage earner may result in a poor investment strategy, as investing is goal-oriented with differing time horizons and a distinct order of importance, as defined by the individual investor. Your advisor should also want to meet with you and your young wage earner at least once per year, as life changes with fair regularity, and along with it, so change objectives, priorities, and dollars available for investing.

3. ***What is the advisor's investment philosophy?*** Regardless of whether you are looking to enlist the services of a full financial

Planner or simply an investment manager, that individual (or the firm with which they work) should have a stated and easily explainable investment philosophy. The philosophy should outline not only the types of investments they select on behalf of their clients, but also their buy/sell/hold decision process, the frequency with which accounts are reviewed, and how, whether or not, and how often they make changes in portfolios. While there are seemingly infinite choices in the investment arena, there are a significantly lower number of those which are appropriate for the typical retail investor. Even if your investable net worth is in the millions, that fact alone should not serve as an indicator of risk appetite or the desire to "get clever" with respect to diversification of your investments.

4. ***What is the client base of the advisor?*** Knowing the age range and types of clients who hire an advisor and continue to work with that individual may prove meaningful, as a lack of familiarity on the part of the advisor with your distinct life stage and circumstances may prove detrimental to you.

You may also wish to build on this with addition questions, including the following:

- ✓ If I work with you as a clients, will you work with my kid on either a free or deeply discounted basis?
- ✓ Do you have any past client complaints or financial disclosures? What do they feel is the reason behind having or not having them?

- ✓ Can you provide me with an example of a time you made what you ultimately felt was a bad investment decision or error with a client? What led you to make that mistake? What did you learn as a result and how has your investment process changed to ensure similar situations are more likely to be avoided?

- ✓ What was your professional experience like during the last economic downturn, and what did you learn from it?

- ✓ How do you feel about increased regulation within the financial industry in general?

- ✓ What drove you to enter into the financial field to begin with? (If the suggestion is that they did it primarily or solely for the money or because they "have always been good at sales," these may be warning signs that they are more concerned with their personal income levels than with bettering the lives and financial positions of their clients, as planning should not equate to selling).

Regardless of how exhaustive the list of questions you pose turns out to be or which specific questions you choose to ask, be sure you have educated yourself to the extent that you are able to determine the meaning, applicability, validity or integrity of the response. Failure to perform sufficient due diligence when considering the fact that this individual will guide you with a substantial number of potentially life-changing financial decisions over the course of your relationship may result in a bad experience at the least, and potential loss of a sizable portion of your nest egg at the worst.

Credit

This may seem like an afterthought, given that it comes last in the fiscal responsibility section; however, this is one of the most important points in the book. You may want to read this section aloud to your young wage earners each night before the drift off to sleep.

All through school, or at least back in the 1970s, as a vague yet somehow terrifying threat, teachers queried rambunctious students with, *"would you like this to go on your Permanent Record...?"* They often let the words trail off, hanging like the Wile E. Coyote past the edge of a cliff, while the student was left pondering what on earth that could mean, knowing that it could not possibly be a good thing.

As it turned out, the illustrious Permanent Record amounted to little more than a banker's box filled with report cards, macaroni art, the occasional bit of school work emblazoned with an A in a circle and a "Well Done!" to emphasize the uniqueness of the performance, and a handful of professionally taken photos reflecting that *all* those years were awkward years. Nothing particularly damning seemed to be present – the time the spelling book was left in the locker; the time not enough chin-ups were executed in P.E., the time the lunch tray was dropped and everyone applauded at the apparent hilarity – none of those was included.

Your credit report, on the other hand, is indeed a permanent record of nearly every financial decision you have made during your lifetime, and will follow you everywhere. Credit reports are reviewed not only by potential lenders (for private student loans, car loans, financing a home purchase, etc.), but also by insurance underwriters (including life, health, and auto), potential landlords, possible future employers, and of course credit card providers, just to name a few. As such, establishing and maintaining an excellent credit rating should be stressed, reinforced, taught, retaught, and then harped on as if it is the lynchpin to all possible future success.

Not only will an excellent credit rating make securing these loans and other life benefits a smoother process, but often results in considerable cost savings as well. Reduced interest rates on loans and lowered premiums on car insurance are perks routinely enjoyed by those with a stellar rating, as a favorable credit rating is seen as not only an indicator of the existence of a financial history, but of actual financial *responsibility* which suggests an overall understanding and acceptance of responsibility in general. A low credit score, on the other hand, is seen as a reflection of a careless attitude towards finances and may warn of similar risk appetites and attitudes with respect to life in general.

Having little or no credit history is often nearly as detrimental as having a low credit score. As such, getting started with responsible behavior early is a good idea, and often begins with the opening of a bank account to understand how to manage personal finances. Things that you or your kid should know about maintaining a bank account in order to develop that understanding include keeping an appropriate account minimum, avoiding overdrafting the account and reconciling the statement on a monthly basis. While the history of the bank account is not reflected on the credit report, good habits are best established early.

Obtaining the first actual credit card should be done under the supervision of the Household Director, and will likely require a cosigner, and is best sought from the bank where the kid maintains the account. The card should be used fairly routinely, paying off the balance in full each month, and used at manageable levels that are easily paid off through Household or other wages. In imparting this wisdom, **stress the importance of that monthly payoff** – this will help avoid the development of the attitude that anything can be had now and then paid over time. Carrying a balance, even on a credit card with a comparatively low interest rate, is expensive over time.

This is not meant to be an exhaustive dissertation on how to develop and nurture your credit rating throughout life, but rather as a way to plant the seed that having and maintaining an excellent credit rating *will* make a difference in life. A simple Google search of "tips to establish good credit" will result in numerous great ideas and strategies, which should be discussed at length with your wage earners.

Fiscal responsibility is an important piece of wisdom you should impart (or obtain), as it plays a substantial role in the likelihood of success for the individual on the receiving end. Those who understand how to earn a dollar, the value of that dollar, what to do with dollars earned and how to protect the resulting nest egg, are better poised to manage their own lives more successfully – be that through the financial strain of college, sudden unforeseen expenses (i.e., a new roof, new appliances, or a new car), or simply of day-to-day life.

Section 5

Preparing for a Household Corporation "Spin-off"

"The last 10% it takes to launch something takes as much energy as the first 90%."

– Rob Kalin, Etsy Founder

Sending your wage earner off into the world can be a stressful and daunting task for any parent, whether financially or emotionally. Hopefully by the time your wage earner is of the age to form their own "Spin-off" corporation, they will be prepared for the endeavor as their "Parent Corporation" has theoretically provided sufficient training to become an independent entity. However, no matter how much they have prepared to leave the nest and fly out on their own, the "first flight" is going to be stressful for both the wage earner as well as the parents. It is this stress that must be overcome by the Parent Corporation so that they can adequately foster the development and growth of the future Director of the Spin Off Corporation.

The key to the success of any Corporation, including a Spin-off corporation, revolves around being able to budget effectively for future goals. As discussed previously in the Fiscal Responsibility Section, one must know the difference between cash flow and budgeting. It is often assumed that by tracking the cash flow of your Household you are, in effect, creating a budget, but this is not the case. The cash flow of a given company is merely a reflection of where all of their dollars are being spent as well as where their inflow of dollars is coming from. Anyone who spends money certainly has a cash flow but not everyone who spends money has a budget. As a poignant reminder, the main difference between the two is that cash flow looks into the past whereas a budget is a plan for the present and future, be that the future of an individual, or an entirely new Spin-off Household.

Ready to Launch

By the time a wage earner (in this example, Warren) is ready to form his own Household Corporation, he should have acquired the skills and income necessary to manage and pay all of his own bills and operate independently from his Parent Corporation. Preparation for a launch should not, however, begin at T-minus ten days to Spin-off, but rather should start at least six months in advance with the development of a timeline for transition.

Consider that Warren not only needs to apprentice those hired to replace him in his household job roles, but he will also need to quickly learn any duties with which he has little to no prior experience, as each job is an essential component of a well-run Household. Warren will also need to look at what he can realistically afford, which means developing an understanding of not only the costs of rent, cellphone and car payments, with which he is already familiar, but all the other expenses associated with running a Household.

It is imperative that the Director work with Warren to create a timetable for the transference of not only his Household job responsibilities, but also to outline as full list of expenses and create an operating budget to

Ready to Launch

ensure a smooth transition both for Warren, as well as for those remaining at home.

Based on his available free time, Warren and the Director agree that he should first focus on apprenticing his younger siblings in his job duties as they relate to his positions as Laundry Manager, Kitchen Maintenance I, and Household IT Manager. The Director posts the jobs and interviews candidates, determining who will assume these roles. Once the new wage earner has accepted the job, Warren will train his successor in the same manner as was done for him upon his initial hire. By handing off those duties to the new hire, Warren then has time to learn any jobs which he has not previously done. Since, for instance, Jimmy has always served in the capacity of the Meal Planning Assistant, Warren has never needed to set a meal plan for the week, determine what groceries need to be purchased or done the grocery shopping.

By learning the jobs of each of his siblings, Warren not only becomes fully proficient in all Household operations, but each member of his family feels they are contributing to the success of Warren's Spin-off.

In addition to learning the required tasks and responsibilities previously covered by the other wage earners, Warren will also need to become proficient in the responsibilities of the Officers of the Household Corporation as well. Officers may elect to sit down individually with Warren, providing him with a lesson on the scope of their responsibilities and their methods for completing them. This is extremely important, as Warren may know how to create a personal budget and stick to it, but he may not even be aware of all the responsibilities the Officers are in charge of, as they often happen "behind the scenes" such as planning for unexpected expenses associated with living independently. As noted, Warren will be responsible for covering all of his own bills and expenses. The Director should work closely with Warren to create his budget and "business plan" for his Spin-off Corporation which the Director should carefully review in order to provide Warren with valuable feedback.

This is particularly crucial because, as anyone who moved out prior to taking on all their own bills can attest, there are bills and expenses that are much more expensive than realized or were even overlooked entirely. Those who move out with initial continued financial support, who then have that support terminated in one fell swoop, learn the hard way that the combined total of the cable/internet, cellphone, gas, electric, water, sewer, and garbage bills may actually amount to nearly half of what they are paying in rent per month. *Running* a household is nearly as expensive as *renting* the Household.

In addition, it is common for those who have never lived independently to fail to consider not only the routine expenses associated with running a Household, but unexpected expenses, like a sudden transmission failure and the subsequent need to purchase a car. Establishing an emergency cash reserve prior to launching the Spin-off may help with unbudgeted, sudden financial surprises.

It is assumed that Warren will not elect to launch until such time as he is gainfully employed, has found reasonable housing and has received his first paycheck.

This can be a transition that takes place over a few weeks, in the case where the wage earner is a salaried employee, or over a few months, when the wage earner is earning minimum wage. In the ideal scenario, the wage earner will be financially independent from the Corporation upon the launch of their Spin-off as that will ensure that there is no "sticker-shock" upon seeing their cell phone bill, or any other bill for that matter, arrive in their mailbox.

Upon the launch of the Spin-Off Corporation, thus marking the end of Warren's employment, he should be provided with a full copy of his employment record, inclusive of all performance reviews, business plans he created, letters of recommendation, complaints filed against him, as well as all versions of his resume. This provides Warren with an historical record on which he can build future versions of his Real World resume as well as numerous keepsakes which he can one day share with the future members of his Household Corporation.

Failure to Launch
(Or the Return of a Wage Earner to the Household Corporation)

In 2016, a study was published by the Pew Research Center which showed that for the age group of 18-34 year olds, 32.1% of individuals were living in their parents' house.

> ("For First Time in Modern Era, Living With Parents Edges Out Other Living Arrangements for 18-34- Year-Olds" Pew Research Center, Washington, D.C. (May 24, 2016) http://www.pewsocialtrends.org/2016/05/24/for-first-time-in-modern-era-living-with-parents-edges-out-other-living-arrangements-for-18-to-34-year-olds/ August 14, 2016)

We are aware that complete independence is not always feasible for every situation and in certain circumstances, a wage earner (in this example, Jimmy) may have to move back home after college or after an unsuccessfully launched Spin-off. Should that situation arise, clear expectations need to be outlined in writing before Jimmy is absorbed back into the Household Corporation. It should be clearly outlined that he is expected to work towards moving out and achieving independence and as such there will be no "free lunch". A contract should be drafted, inclusive of the terms under which Jimmy will be permitted to be reabsorbed into the Household Corporation. That contract should include, but is not limited to the following:

Rent payment – It must be clear that Jimmy understands he will pay rent and the monthly amount will be set in stone. Rental premiums should increase on an annual basis to ensure Jimmy does not become complacent with cheap living arrangements. Rental increases will help offset any

Ready to Launch

rising Household costs associated with inflation, but will additionally serve as an incentive for Jimmy to relaunch his Spin-off.

Contribution towards household expenses – It should be determined to what extent or percentage of the Household expenses Jimmy will be responsible for while he is living within the household. He must help out financially with groceries, utility bills, as well as covering 100% of his own expenses, such as gas, insurance and his car payment. By outlining, in detail, all of the expenses he is responsible for covering, it ensures the Director does not fall prey to Jimmy's constant desire to receive ongoing support without end.

Leisure vs Work: Another point that must be addressed in the contract is setting an appropriate expectation for Jimmy with regards to outside employment. This should include not only how many hours he will be expected to work, but in the event his job is not a permanent one (i.e., part-time fast food employee versus a professional fulltime salaried position), the number of jobs for which he will be expected to apply and interview. In addition, a clear timeframe in which he will be expected to accept a position in his chosen field should be clearly outlined. This will ensure that upon graduating high school or college, Jimmy does not "take a gap year" to play video games on the couch all day, which presents the opportunity to snowball into a considerably longer timeframe, as he becomes farther and farther removed from his previously set goals and his attained education.

Curfew, Quiet Hours and Waking Hours: A clear schedule of designated Household quiet hours, when Jimmy is expected to be home for the night, as well as expected waking hours should be outlined in the contract. If

Preparing for a Household Corporation "Spin-Off"

Jimmy is a responsible adult who has simply fallen on hard times, the need for a curfew may not exist; however, if he is of the mindset that he is entitled to a "gap year," or that he will finds a job *someday*, late-night comings and goings may prove disruptive to the normal flow of Household operations and may interfere with the quiet time that should be afforded other Household members. Irrespective of establishing a curfew, quiet hours, as well as waking hours must be established. Consider that Jimmy is reabsorbed into the Household Corporation and gets a job at a fast food restaurant working the night shift. He arrives home just after 2:00 a.m. and wants to unwind after his shift. Once home, he decides he will fix a snack so he heads to the kitchen to cook a pizza. Morgan, his sister whose bedroom is just off the kitchen, is awakened by the clatter outside her room and now must either confront Jimmy, which may lead to an altercation, or she can resign herself to a restless night without much sleep. This situation is further exacerbated when members of the household share a room and there is no way to avoid sleep disruption.

Due to his late return home, followed by a pizza and an hour spent unwinding at the video game console, Jimmy will be inclined to sleep much later than the other Household members. While he may have some expectation that the Household will remain quiet until he stirs, it must be made clear that Household Operations commence for the day at a certain time and Household members are not going to remain silent while Jimmy sleeps past noon, regardless of the circumstances. Household members must not need to walk on eggs shells in order to accommodate the incompatible work and leisure schedule of the returned individual.

By clearly outlining at the outset the Household quiet hours and hours of activity, disruption to the normal flow of the environment can be addressed in a constructive manner as opposed to the issue escalating into a shouting match, between members of the Household.

Timeframe for Departure: At the outset of the agreement, it should be made clear that the agreement will not go on indefinitely. A clear timeframe should be established for the creation of the Jimmy's next Spin-off corporation (i.e., he is definitely going to have to move out). This timeframe can certainly be adjusted based on unforeseen or extenuating circumstances, but the Director should avoid the trap of continuously finding excuses to permit Jimmy to remain in the Parent Corporation. Many parents are too kind-hearted to forcibly shove their little bird from the nest, but for some, without that nudge, they simply will never launch. As the deadline for the timeframe approaches, it should be reiterated to Jimmy that he is expected to be self-sustaining by the deadline and progress checks will need to be made throughout his stay to ensure that he is on track to meet that deadline.

While a Spin-off may present a highly emotional situation for all members of the Household Corporation, it must be remembered that the goal in having kids is to ultimately launch them as successful, functional, contributing members of society. This may not always be the desire of every Household member; however, it is certainly in the best interest of the personal growth and future success of the individual being launched. Educating kids and instilling in them a fundamental understanding of what goes into establishing and running a Household will likely not only result in a greater appreciation of the Director's commitment to the Household, but a deeper understanding of the tremendous amount of work that goes into running a successful one.

Section 6
Writing the Real Deal Resume
(and a great cover letter)

"Resume: a written exaggeration of only the good things a person has done in the past, as well as a wish list of the qualities a person would like to have."

– Robert "Beau" Bennett, Author and Entrepreneur

Writing a resume that reflects your unique skills and capabilities takes some thoughtful consideration. When many people embark on writing a resume, they generally start with a chronological account of the jobs they have held and a small sampling of the duties they were assigned while in that position. As those same individuals make their way up the ladder of their given field, they may choose to include additional details, such as projects on which they worked jointly with a team, awards and other recognition received, and milestones met. They then add their professional goal statement, their computer skills (i.e., I have a good working knowledge of the internet), a couple personal points (i.e., I love the outdoors and I'm a real people-person), and ultimately close with **References Available Upon Request.**

Following is the actual resume submitted to me by my coauthor in consideration for employment; he has reluctantly agreed to permit the printing and subsequent mocking of this for the purposes of the betterment of resumes as a whole.

Brett Pawelkiewicz

Objective
I hope to obtain a position with a well established organization with a stable environment that will lead to a long lasting relationship in the management field

Experience

8/2008 – 8/2013   Windy City Clean Up   Fox River Grove, IL
(Seasonal)
Supervisor of Midway Operations
- Managing Payroll and Budgeting expenses
- Organizing and Managing a Team of six workers
- Running Day to Day operations

5/102010 – 8/2013   Model Cleaning Co.   Roselle, IL
Model cleaner
- Cleaning the exterior and interior of model homes at 3 communities
- Maintaining and ensuring models stay clean
- Managing and purchasing supplies

10/2013 – 01/2014   B&B Holiday Decorating   Des Plaines , IL
Crew Leader
- Taking inventory and managing supply needs
- Creating and designing installation plans for new customers
- Installing and maintaining holiday lights with a crew of 2-3 workers

Education

8/2009 – 5/2012   University of Illinois Champaign/Urbana   Champaign, IL
Economics
- With a concentration in Physics

Skills and Strengths

Communication: Good verbal and written presentation skills
Interpersonal skills: Able to get along well with co-workers and accept supervision
Attention to Detail: Concerned with quality and ensuring tasks are completed correctly and on time
Leadership skills: Can work with many different personalities and motivate individuals towards a common goal
Time and Project management: Can efficiently manage time in order to reach project goals
Flexible: Willing to learn new methods to improve efficiency when completing tasks

References Available Upon Request

There are two inherent problems with this type of resume.

First, it only looks backwards and gives no indication of what the candidate might be capable of in the future. While looking into the rear view mirror is helpful to know how far you have come, with any luck, the future is far more interesting and worth heading towards. Resumes should be written with forward, and indeed upward, momentum in mind. Getting stuck in the same types of roles throughout your career can break your spirit and your desire to move on to new challenges, especially if time and time again, those efforts seem to go unrewarded, unappreciated or worse – unnoticed. Your resume should get you noticed, and that holds true whether you happen to be 8 or 58.

Second, this type of resume lists the *tasks* you have done and separately tacks on the underlying skills required to master those tasks, almost as an afterthought. While this may seem similar or even a reiteration of what we have just said, and they do go hand in hand, that is not the case – failing to attach the underlying skills directly to the mastered tasks for each job makes it appear as if the list of skills was copied directly from an internet resume template and hints at the fact that the candidate may not actually possess those skills. Had the skills been connected directly to the job experience, the resume would have shown how the candidate *applied* their skillset when facing various challenges and opportunities, thereby indicating an understanding of how those same skills may be applied in the future to achieve similar or still more impressive successes.

Fixing both of these issues starts and ends in the same place – with critical thinking that may need to take place outside the box. How far outside the box you elect to go is often determined by your creativity, your desire to move up whatever corporate (or other type of) ladder you are climbing, your self-confidence and your dogged commitment to your own personal and professional growth.

Now, before you put this book down while ranting about how much you hate the term "outside the box" and everything it represents, please keep in mind that we are not encouraging anyone to pursue something outside of their own interests (unless of course, they want to!), or to fabricate a series of, albeit impressive, falsehoods, but rather to look at their skillset perhaps in a way they had never thought to previously. The simple goal is creating a more accurate representation of that which you are uniquely capable.

In the interest of saving space, we should move on.

When applying for a new job, most people begin their search with the job that they *have*, rather than the job they *want*. While this ensures that person will easily be able to transition into the new role with little time or necessity for training or orientation (aside from perhaps locating the community coffee pot and the restroom), what it fails to do is to move that person forward. The issue with this is that the set of circumstances that put the individual on the path of seeking out a new job may become a reality in the new job as well, despite the fact that the commute is ten minutes shorter, the pay is slightly better or the people are more agreeable at the outset. Eventually, you will hit traffic, the raises will seem out of proportion with your increased workload and okay, maybe the people will still be cool, but should those people move on to other jobs, you may inherit their workload – essentially landing you right back on square one.

A good job search begins with what you actually want to do, which may not be what you have historically done. Careful consideration of what you actually want to do requires far more effort than recalling the dates you worked as a cashier at Target during college, and may even require some personal discovery. We strongly suggest starting with the things you know you definitely do *not* like to do, based on the jobs or responsibilities you have had up until this new job search. That may look something like this:

<u>Stuff I really don't like doing</u>
- I don't like working in a cubicle where everyone can interrupt me as they please
- I don't like doing the same set of tasks in the same order every day
- I don't like working on something for the first two thirds of a project only to have to hand off my best work and see it altered without my consent
- I don't like others getting credit for my contributions
- I don't like being tied to a desktop computer and not having the ability to work remotely
- I don't like the mundane nature of bookkeeping
- I don't like being held accountable for the performance of members of my team, despite the fact that I'm not given any authority to incentivize or discipline my team

Since nearly everyone dislikes some aspect of their job, we recommend that you take that same list and work through it to determine which of those things could still comprise 20% of your time without otherwise compromising your morale.

<u>Stuff I could tolerate doing if everything else is good</u>
- I could handle working in a cubicle, so long as it's in a remote part of the office and I'm allowed to let people

know that they can't interrupt me while I'm working on a certain project
- I could work on part of a project provided my input is sought when someone higher up feels the need to change what I've done (sometimes it just seems like they missed the point of my whole design)
- I could work on a desktop computer if I am allowed to get/use my own laptop for work

Then, take the time to think about things you actually enjoy. Not necessarily those things that involve your job, but those types of things you enjoy. This is the outside the box part...

<u>Stuff I enjoy doing</u>
- I like being outdoors
- I like helping people
- I like feeling heard
- I like solving puzzles
- I like working in a team, but not being the lead

These concepts might initially seem completely inapplicable to any job search, but consider that the job you are leaving behind (in this case, bookkeeping) is being done in a cubicle, as the leader of a team of unmotivated and inefficient workers, with little authority and clearly no opportunity to shine as an individual. If you choose to revamp your resume, you should specifically gear it towards obtaining a job that has you traveling to a number of different clients, solving complex bookkeeping problems (this is, after all, your field of expertise), being in charge of your own flexible schedule and ideally having the opportunity to fulfill a number of your personal "likes" in the process of working what has otherwise proven to be a dull and uninspiring job to you.

Going back to my coauthor's resume, it should be noted that the *format* of the document is certainly clean, easy to read and appealing, and you, the new Outside the Box thinker, may choose to utilize that same format to first present your new career objective, which reads: *"To obtain a position offering challenging short-term bookkeeping assignments which need great concentration and insight to solve. The ideal position will have a travel component and offer me the flexibility to create my own schedule."* Simply putting this to paper may provide you sufficient motivation to drop this in every available in-box to which you can gain access. It very clearly states what you are looking for in a job and conveys a measure of excitement at the prospect of doing this type of work.

Fleshing out the experience section of a resume should not be approached solely from the perspective of date and duty recall. Describing your employment history should speak to a selection of accomplishments of which you are most proud. You may elect to refer to additional accomplishments in a cover letter, alluding to the fact that had you listed everything you had done on your resume, you may have been forced to sacrifice listing the applicability of meaningful skills in order to conserve space, which you felt would have reflected poorly on your understanding of the fundamental basis of your own successes.

Referring back to the sample resume, following is an example of how to apply the listed skills to the outlined job responsibilities:

2/2008 – 8/2013   Windy City Clean Up   Fox River Grove, IL
(Seasonal)

Supervisor of Midway Operations

Despite the seasonal nature of my employment with Windy City Clean Up, and due to my demonstrated high level of understanding of the accounting process, I was afforded the opportunity to expand my responsibilities from simply maintenance in nature to managing the payroll process and budgeting various operational expenses on behalf of the company.

In addition, over six consecutive summers, my loyalty and commitment to the highest standard of work, were rewarded with a promotion to managing and organizing the work schedule and flow for a staff of six individuals. My demonstrated leadership and ability to manage and motivate workers with widely varied personalities and communication skills ultimately led to being entrusted with the task of running all day-to-day operations.

While this fundamentally states exactly what was listed on the original resume, the candidate shows not only that of which he is capable, but that he is loyal, dedicated, has a strong work ethic, is trustworthy, able to manage and lead despite his youth, and is upwardly motivated. Moreover, this wording suggests the candidate truly understands why he was granted responsibility at the level he was and therefore will likely be able to apply those same skills to take on new tasks of ever-increasing levels of importance and difficulty.

Ready to Launch

If you list your skills and strengths in this manner – within the framework of your work experience – there is no need to reiterate those skills in list format. Instead this space should be reserved for an impressive list of technical abilities, such as the ability to type at a certain speed, a flair for designing computer-based presentations, or experience with job-specific software packages.

Your education should reflect not only your degree, but also your interests, and this is where you may choose to include a personal data point or two in order to spark the curiosity of a potential future boss by possibly listing a shared interest which may ultimately lead to a more personalized and therefore relaxed interview. Save the **References Available Upon Request** for the cover letter, however, which should be simple, professional, respectful and concise.

A sample cover letter might look like this:

September 1, 2016

Mr. Alexander J. Fitzpatrick
Director of Human Resources
NBP Reliant Services
789 Main Street
Bradley, IL 60915

RE: **Job Opportunity Inquiry**

Dear Mr. Fitzpatrick,

I am writing to respectfully submit the enclosed resume in consideration for your recently-posted opening with your traveling bookkeeping services division. While my resume reflects

22 years in the field of accounting, I want to add that the nature of the position as I understand it, speaks specifically to my desire to obtain a position that varies from day-to-day, offers me a challenging workload and carries with it the expectation of travel. I feel that these combined factors will inspire me to work to the top of my ability, with impeccable attention to detail, speed and efficiency, as not only do I feel I am professionally qualified for the position, but the nature of the work will bring me considerable joy and a renewed sense of energy and excitement about my job.

I would very sincerely appreciate the opportunity to interview with you for this position and to have the chance to engage in a deeper discovery of this extremely unique opportunity. Should you elect to afford me that opportunity, I will be happy to provide you with a list of professional references, inclusive of coworkers, subordinates, and those who have supervised me directly.

Kind thanks to you, in advance, for your consideration.
Very truly,

Grace
Grace Alexis

By taking the time to think through writing a resume that truly speaks to not only your education but to your personal interests as well (to the extent possible), searching for a job, and indeed applying for a job, may become less of a chore and more of an exciting opportunity. Submitting your resume for consideration, knowing that given the chance to sit down with that person, you are certain to impress, will provide you with a greater sense of self-satisfaction. This may also reveal and honor who you are, what you enjoy, how you are motivated and the full scope of your unique set of skills and innate talents.

Now get outside the box, explore who you are and find the job of your dreams!

Appendix

The Smith Household Corporation
Kitchen Maintenance I – Job Description

The person selected for this position will be responsible for the cleanliness of the kitchen and dining room areas as well as ensuring that all required supplies are in stock.

Primary Responsibilities

- Ensuring all dirty dishes are promptly washed and put away
- Pre-soaking and scrubbing any pots and pans that may require it
- Keeping the kitchen sink empty of all dirty dishes to ensure that it can be used when the Executive Chef is preparing meals
- Cleaning any and all surfaces in the kitchen area
- Sweeping and Mopping the kitchen floors on a weekly basis
- Communicating any supply needs to the Meal Planning Assistant to ensure that they are purchased before they run out
- Cleaning the table before and/or after a meal
- Checking the refrigerator on a weekly basis to ensure all spoiled food is discarded
- Cleaning the refrigerator on a weekly basis
- Ensuring any and all kitchen appliances are clean and in working order (i.e. microwave, toaster over, dish washer etc.)

Requirements

- Cleanliness
- Attention to detail
- Timeliness in completing job tasks as dishes that sit too long may start to emit foul odors
- Ability to communicate with others
- Ability to function in a loud and sometimes chaotic work environment
- Willingness to get "dirty"

Career Path

- Gain sufficient understanding of the cleaning process to eventually use these skills to take on the job of Bathroom Maintenance as well as any other positions which require cleaning
- Develop a "cleanliness is next to godliness" mentality such that cleaning up after themselves will be second nature and will not require extra effort on their part

Compensation

- Base Wage: $X
- Hours: Will vary based on number wage earners in the corporation as this will directly affect the number of items that need to be cleaned
- Bonus opportunities will be determined based upon the extracurricular activities and interests of the individual hired for this position

The Smith Household Corporation
Laundry Manager – Job Description

The person selected for this position will be responsible for ensuring all laundry needs are met and for ensuring all corporate wage earners have clean laundry, as well as ensuring all required supplies are in stock.

Primary Responsibilities

- Create the systems and processes by which all corporate wage earners need to abide by in order to ensure their laundry is completed.
    - How dirty laundry will be collected by the Head of Laundry Operations
    - How stains or special instructions should be communicated to the Head of Laundry Operations
    - How rush requests should be submitted and the stipulations around such requests (i.e. three rush requests per year with a minimum of six hours notice)
    - How clean laundry will be returned to the wage earner.
- Develop and maintain a laundry schedule for all corporate wage earners
- Communicating the laundry schedule to all corporate wage earners and informing them of any and all updates to the schedule
- Ensuring all required supplies are in stock
- Coordinating with the Meal Planning Assistant to ensure all required supplies are purchased when supplies are low.
- Collecting all dirty laundry on at least a weekly basis
- Sorting dirty laundry to ensure all garments are washed in an appropriate manner (i.e. separating dark colors and light colors, dry hanging any clothes that cannot be put into the dryer)
- Washing all dirty laundry
- Ensuring all washed laundry is dried in an appropriate manner (hang dry vs machine dry)
- Ironing clothes as necessary (provided they are mature enough to handle an iron)
- Folding clothes in a neat and orderly manner
- Placing all folded laundry in their respective laundry baskets and returning them to their wage earners.

Requirements

- Ability to organize and sort objects with many different properties
- Ability to remain flexible in order to ensure all rush requests are fulfilled
- Being able to plan ahead and to determine what supplies may be needed when special events are coming up
- Punctuality and prompt performance of duties according to the set laundry schedule
- Ability to demonstrate patience and tact with other wage earners when rush requests are submitted
- Ability to communicate with all wage earners and ensure that all of their requirements are known
- Ability to coordinate and work with many different schedules, some of which may be hectic and subject to change frequently.

Career Path

- Gain sufficient organizational and procedural skills to grow with the role as wage earners join extracurricular activities; eventually increasing those skills in order to move on to a wage position which bears more responsibility (i.e. Household Financial Assistant, Meal Planning Assistant, etc.)
- Developing the skills necessary to handle all laundry related tasks when living along

Compensation

- Base Wage: $X
- Hours: Will vary based on number of wage earners as well as their wardrobe size and needs
- Bonus opportunities will be determined based upon the extracurricular activities and interests of the individual hired for this position

Director's Performance Evaluation Questionnaire

Wage Earner's Name: _____
Review Period: _____ to _____
Date of Review: _____

Please provide thoughtful responses to the following questions; the information you provide will be used to help the Director improver the operations of the Household Corporation to ensure a healthy and fair work environment, as well as to further efforts to foster the growth of all wage earners. Please submit your completed self-evaluation questionnaire to the Director no later than two weeks prior to your next performance review.

Part 1: Performance Appraisal

1. What suggestions do you have for the Director in order to increase productivity and team morale?
   _____
   _____

2. In what areas has the Director had exceptional performance? Provide specific examples.
   _____
   _____

3. In which areas does the Director need to focus more attention or improve? Provide specific examples.
   _____
   _____

4. What additional rewards or incentives would you like to see added to the compensation package?
   _____
   _____

5. Have there been instances where you feel misconduct was handled unfairly? Provide specific examples.
   _____
   _____

6. What can the Director – and the Household Corporation as a whole – do to help ensure that you are making progress toward accomplishing our professional development goals?
   _____
   _____

Part 2: Performance Ratings:

1. How would you rate their performance based on *consistency*?

1	2	3	4	5
Unsatisfactory	Needs Improvement	Meets Expectations	Satisfactory	Exceeds Expectations

2. How would you rate their performance based on *fairness*?

1	2	3	4	5
Unsatisfactory	Needs Improvement	Meets Expectations	Satisfactory	Exceeds Expectations

3. How would you rate their performance in *handling misconduct/bad-behavior*?

1	2	3	4	5
Unsatisfactory	Needs Improvement	Meets Expectations	Satisfactory	Exceeds Expectations

4. How would you rate their performance in *setting wages*?

1	2	3	4	5
Unsatisfactory	Needs Improvement	Meets Expectations	Satisfactory	Exceeds Expectations

5. How would you rate their overall attitude towards all wage earner's job duties?

1	2	3	4	5
Unsatisfactory	Needs Improvement	Meets Expectations	Satisfactory	Exceeds Expectations

Part 3: Additional Comments

Please provide any additional comments or suggestions that you would like to share.

_____
_____
_____

Submitted By:

Date: _____

_____
Wage Earner's Name (Please print)

_____
Signature

Wage Earner Performance Evaluation Questionnaire

Wage Earner's Name: _____
Review Period: _____ to _____
Date of Review: _____

Please provide thoughtful responses to the following questions; the information you provide will be used to help wage earners improve their current responsibilities as well as aid them in taking on additional responsibilities. Please complete the Wage Earner Performance Evaluation at least two weeks prior to the performance review.

Part 1: Performance Appraisal

1. What skills and traits have been exhibited by the wage earner during this last review period? How do you see these skills and traits helping them during their professional life?
_____
_____
_____

2. What areas of their duties have they had exceptional performance in? Provide specific examples.
_____
_____
_____

3. What areas of their duties do they need to focus more attention on or improve? Provide specific examples.
_____
_____
_____

4. What additional responsibilities/job duties has the wage earner taken on since the last performance review?
_____
_____
_____

5. What can the wage earner do to ensure that the Household Corporation is progressing and operating more efficiently?
_____
_____
_____

6. What goals or responsibilities would you like to see the wage earner achieve during the next performance period?
_____
_____
_____

Part 2: Performance Ratings:

How would you rate their job performance based on *consistency*?

1	2	3	4	5
Unsatisfactory	Needs Improvement	Meets Expectations	Satisfactory	Exceeds Expectations

How would you rate their job performance based on *reliability*?

1	2	3	4	5
Unsatisfactory	Needs Improvement	Meets Expectations	Satisfactory	Exceeds Expectations

How would you rate their job performance based on *willingness to take on additional responsibilities*?

1	2	3	4	5
Unsatisfactory	Needs Improvement	Meets Expectations	Satisfactory	Exceeds Expectations

How would you rate their job performance in terms of *begin a team player*?

1	2	3	4	5
Unsatisfactory	Needs Improvement	Meets Expectations	Satisfactory	Exceeds Expectations

How would you rate their job performance based on *organization*?

1	2	3	4	5
Unsatisfactory	Needs Improvement	Meets Expectations	Satisfactory	Exceeds Expectations

How would you rate their job performance based on *technical skills*?

1	2	3	4	5
Unsatisfactory	Needs Improvement	Meets Expectations	Satisfactory	Exceeds Expectations

Part 3: Additional Comments

Please provide any additional comments or suggestions that you would like to share.

_____
_____
_____

Submitted By:					Date: _____

_____			_____
Director's Name (Please print)			Signature

Employee Self Evaluation Questionnaire

Wage Earner's Name: _____
Review Period: _____ to _____
Date of Review: _____

Please provide thoughtful responses to the following questions; the information you provide will be used to help develop your performance goals as well as your personal goals for the next performance period. Please submit your completed self-evaluation questionnaire to the Director no later than two weeks prior to your next performance review.

Part 1: Job Development

1. What have you done since your last review to improve as related to your current position and future goals with the Household Corporation?

2. What outcomes and improvements have you seen as a result of the actions described above?

3. What projects and accomplishments from the past year are you most proud of?

4. What goals would you like to set for yourself to accomplish during the next review period?

5. What additional responsibilities and/or job duties have you taken on since the last review?

Part 2: Performance Ratings:

How would you rate your job performance based on *consistency*? Is the quality of your work always the same?

1	2	3	4	5
Unsatisfactory	Needs Improvement	Meets Expectations	Satisfactory	Exceeds Expectations

How would you rate your job performance based on *reliability*? Do you always do your job?

1	2	3	4	5
Unsatisfactory	Needs Improvement	Meets Expectations	Satisfactory	Exceeds Expectations

How would you rate your job performance based on *willingness to take on additional responsibilities?*

1	2	3	4	5
Unsatisfactory	Needs Improvement	Meets Expectations	Satisfactory	Exceeds Expectations

How would you rate your job performance in terms of *being a team player*?

1	2	3	4	5
Unsatisfactory	Needs Improvement	Meets Expectations	Satisfactory	Exceeds Expectations

How would you rate your job performance based on *organization*?

1	2	3	4	5
Unsatisfactory	Needs Improvement	Meets Expectations	Satisfactory	Exceeds Expectations

How would you rate your job performance based on *technical skills*?

1	2	3	4	5
Unsatisfactory	Needs Improvement	Meets Expectations	Satisfactory	Exceeds Expectations

Part 3: Additional Comments

Please provide any additional comments or suggestions that you would like to share.

_____
_____
_____

Submitted By: Date: _____

_____   _____
Wage Earner's Name (Please print)   Signature

Priority Request Form

Requester's Name: _____

Date of Request: _____

Date Request Needed by: _____

What Item/Duty needs to be made a priority? _____

What Wage-Earner is currently responsible for completing those duties? _____

What is the reason for the increase in priority?
_____
_____
_____

What steps will you take to ensure that this request will not need to have an increased priority moving forward?
_____
_____
_____

Additional Comments:
_____
_____
_____

For Director Use Only

___ Request Granted   ___ Request Denied

Reason for approval/disapproval:
_____
_____

_____   _____
Director's Name   Signature

_____
Date

Savings Match and Vesting Worksheet

Depositor's Name: _____   Match Forfeiture Period: _____

Vesting Schedule: _____   Matching Percentage: _____

Date When Fully Vested: _____

Date	Earner's Savings Deposit	Household Match (10%)	Total Deposit	Date Match is available for Withdrawal

Special Thanks...

*to John Groleau;
without you, this book may never have come to fruition.*

From Dina:

...this book was twelve years in the making, and I want to thank my inspiring co-author for bringing it all together with me; Brett, you have given me the gift of enduring belief and dedicated hard work, when all you really wanted to do was play kan-jam with your friends and family; I will never be able to sufficiently thank you. I also want to thank my parents, Dwight and Marti Lucia, for holding me to the highest expectations possible, instilling in me my undying work ethic, and teaching me that if I grab myself by my britches, I can rise to anything. Thanks also to my sister, Carmen, for being the other half of my "us" and for knowing my guts like no other. Thank you to all the incredible people who willingly shared with me your lives, your trials, your stories, your experiences and your time – would that I had space to note you all by name.

From Brett:

I would like to thank my friend Sean, my nieces Amber and Grace, and their mother Amanda for finding the time in their busy schedules to be the models for our cover art. To all of my siblings, Nick, Scott, Brad, Jordan, Megan, Jack, and Lexi, I couldn't imagine life without any of you in it and couldn't be happier that we get to experience all of life's adventures together. To my parents, Paul, Lisa and John, your enduring patience and love through the evolution of our amazing family has been nothing short of incredible. I will never be able to thank you all enough for everything that you have done for me as words cannot convey my love and appreciation for you. To my grandparents Ron and Jean Pawelkiewicz, and John and Karen Kamin, your never ending supply of love and wisdom has shaped me into the man I am today. You have always been there when anyone has needed you and you have taught me that nothing is more important than family. To the memory of my great-grandparents, Ronald and Ruth Shafer, there will never be anyone like them and if there was, the world would be a better place. And last but certainly not least, I want to thank my co-author Dina for somehow knowing that there was more to me than the nine bullet points listed on my resume. You have provided me with opportunities that I could only have dreamed of and I cannot think of a better partner to change the world with.